BEING A MAN

BEING A MAN

The Paradox of Masculinity

Donald H. Bell

A Harvest/HBJ Book
Harcourt Brace Jovanovich, Publishers
San Diego New York London

Requests for permission to make copies of any part of the work should be mailed to: Permissions, Harcourt Brace Jovanovich, Publishers, Orlando, FL 32887

LIBRARY OF CONGRESS CATALOGING IN PUBLICATION DATA

Bell, Donald H., 1943–
Being a man.

Includes bibliographical references.
1. Bell, Donald H., 1943– . 2. Men—United States—Biography.
3. Sex role—United States. 4. Marriage—United States.
5. Work—Psychological aspects. 6. Father and child. I. Title.
HQ1090.3.B44 305.3'1'0973 82-7196

ISBN 0-15-611686-3 (Harvest/HBJ : pbk.)

First Harvest/HBJ edition 1984

A B C D E F G H I J

For Sara,
with love;
For Zachary and Jonah,
with hope;
And For The Men
In This Book.

CONTENTS

ACKNOWLEDGMENTS

More people than I can possibly mention have helped me with this book. I would like, first of all, to thank all the men who allowed me to probe into their lives and who struggled to make clear the issues and dilemmas which they face. In addition, I would like to offer special thanks to Frank, Beau, Pam, Norm, Bob, John C., Jeff, Kim, Alan, Paula, David, and Toots. The support, love, and (sometimes) the criticism of these friends has helped to sustain the "men's book" through bad days and good. I would like to thank Michael V. Miller for his perceptive comments and for an understanding of the demons with which writers must contend. The staff and management of The Lewis Publishing Company did much to sharpen my thoughts and to clarify my prose: my special thanks to Thomas Begner, Jon Freedman, and Kathy Shulga. I would like to express my gratitude, as well, to Priscilla Miller, who typed one of the first drafts of this manuscript.

My family has done much to sustain me through my time of research and writing. My two brothers have been especially encouraging, although they have as yet seen little of this manuscript. Perhaps now they will understand what all the fuss was about.

Finally, this book would have been impossible to write without Sara's constant love, help, and attention. In a way, this is her book as well as mine. My gratitude to her is without bounds.

I should note that the name of every person in this book other than Sara and myself has been changed. This has been necessary in order to protect the confidences of those who saw fit to speak with me about their lives and about what it means to be a man.

INTRODUCTION

I know my heart and understand my fellow man.

—Jean Jacques Rousseau,
The Confessions

I began to write this book when my marriage ended, one casualty of the changes which had come to men and women in the last decade. Since the end of the 1960s Rachel and I had lived intensely through the various stages of the women's movement and its push for more equal work, a greater division of labor at home, and a more caring sexuality. We struggled together through some unbearably difficult moments and learned much from friends who were negotiating the same uncharted landscape. We shared in the birth and infancy of our son in ways which our parents had never imagined when raising their own children, and we tried to change our ideas and expectations about careers and productive labor. All the while, we prided ourselves on being the "perfect couple," and once we even went on television as an example of "liberated" life-styles. Finally, we could change no further together. Deep inside, I felt like a hostage to plans and events which were out of my control, and Rachel saw me as a jailer who held her captive to an oppressive past. During a matter of months we broke apart in a paroxysm of anger and resentment, destroying all we had tried to accomplish as a couple.

Not long afterward, I lost my teaching job at a leading east coast educational institution, and I found myself faced with a crisis of both love and work—those two persistent poles which in Freud's words are the guideposts of meaning in one's life. Stipulations concerning "affirmative action" and the hiring of women helped contribute to my job loss and this seemed ironic. I had worked hard in my marriage and personal life to help realize the ideals of "affirmative action," and at times I had compromised my own career goals to make equality more possible. Now I was forced to re-examine my actions and beliefs. Even more, I needed to look closely at myself as a man, and especially as a man who had supported women in their struggle, but who now felt deeply wounded by some of the gains of that struggle. I wanted to find out how other men were faring, and I decided to speak with my contemporaries to see what changes the events of the last tumultuous decade had made in their sense of themselves, their feelings about their masculinity, and their expectations for the future. Had men actually changed? What were the gains and losses of readjusting their sense of malehood? What resentments and fears did they harbor? What were the joys and rewards of change?

As I talked with these men, I began to realize that many of them shared my own feelings. To be sure, there were men who rejected the idea of more sexual equality. Feminist novels and treatises abounded with them, and one often encountered stereotypical Archie Bunkers in an older generation or even met young Archies in locker room conversation or saw their traces on bathroom walls. I found, however, that many men in their twenties, thirties, and forties had begun to change their attitudes and behavior. They no longer seemed comfortable with traditional stereotypes: they took pride in sharing their feelings and fears with women or even with other men; they seemed not to be antagonized by sexual equality at their jobs, and many of them were glad not to be saddled with the rigidity of earlier roles and expectations.

The feelings of many of these same men were marked, however, by ambivalence. Even though a generation of males had begun to change their attitudes and actions, some nagging doubts remained. I was told, for example, by a teacher in his mid-thirties that "it's a difficult time to be a man. . . . I still carry traditional expectations about a man's role in the family and being a breadwinner and a 'father figure,' but I also want to develop my affective and feeling side and to assume equal responsibility in the house. Yet, I can't do this all at once. . . . Ultimately, I feel good about changing in the ways my wife has requested, but it also creates a strain. I feel pulled in different directions, and I am often on the defensive."

And a lawyer in his twenties posed another side of the question. "I realize that there are contradictions in my beliefs and attitudes," he said. "I don't mind being equal with women at work, but I still believe in a fairly traditional division of labor at home. I still think that despite everything, women should take care of the house and make dinner. I know that this sounds a little or even a lot like bullshit, but I still take pleasure in it. In a way," this man concludes, "the women's movement has even *increased* my expectations for women. I want them to make dinner, to clean up, *and* to be successful professionally."

It seemed clear that while men had begun to change their lives and were less driven to fulfill traditional male stereotypes, the process of change was slow, often contradictory, and sometimes painful. I learned that contemporary men are usually not the unfeeling cartoon villains of recent feminist fiction, but I also realized that they are not citizens of a new world of virtue. Whatever change has come to the relations of men and women has been halting and has been bought at the price of deeply divided feelings. This has mainly occurred because men have not been prepared by earlier experience for the demands of the last decade. The images of the past die hard, and men who have attempted to change their lives have confronted resistance which has originated as much from within themselves as from the outside world. This, I believe, is the paradox of contemporary masculinity: we are caught between old ways and new, between the era in which we grew up and the time in which we now live.

This book is a kind of progress report on recent changes in the lives of men. It looks essentially at white, middle-class males (many of them in professional occupations) and is based on more than a hundred interviews with subjects drawn from this group. Such a group, of course, is rather restricted and even privileged. I have chosen to speak about these men because I know them better than I know others, and because they might carry the seeds of change to others in our society. I am convinced that the attitudes of the men in this book are beginning to characterize many other American men, and that the process of change will not be confined to a single social group. I am also convinced that the ambivalent feelings about which I speak can be understood as a part of the process of change.[1]

Several kinds of books on men are available. Some have discussed the stages of adult male development and have been concerned with establishing the pace and the framework of individual growth. These books have helped make it clear that change is a continuous and expected part of the life cycle. Daniel Levinson, principal author of *The Seasons of a Man's Life*, argues for example that "everyone lives through the same developmental periods in adulthood, just as in childhood. . . . The concept of life structure—the basic pattern or design of a person's life at a given time—gives us a way of looking at the engagement of the individual in society."[2] And George Vaillant, author of *Adaptation to Life,* in a discussion of the ways in which men cope with stress during different phases of their lives, has this to say: "Adults change over time. If we view lives prospectively, they look different from our retrospective view of them. We were never the little butterflies we imagined. . . . Yet, if we follow adults for years, we can uncover startling changes and evolutions. We can discover developmental discontinuities in adults that are as great as the difference in personality between a nine-year-old and what he becomes at fifteen. . . . The study of lifetimes is comparable to the study of celestial navigation. Neither a sextant nor a celestial map can predict where we *should* go; but both are invaluable in letting us identify where we *are.*[3]

While these authors have departed from the earlier notion that adulthood is a relatively static state to be endured after the tumult of childhood and adolescence, they have been limited by the fact that they have not often related their findings to current changes in the social roles and behavior of men and women, nor have they often described the actual "lived" quality of men's lives. They have not generally understood that stages of development are conditioned by wider shifts in society, and that what was an acceptable series of steps to manhood (or womanhood) a short while ago might not be so acceptable today or tomorrow.

Other authors have treated men in a rather stereotyped fashion. They have criticized men for behaving in outmoded and sexist ways and for hanging on to "macho" images of themselves. Such books have made men aware of the continuing influence of traditional male behavior and have pleaded for greater sensitivity and caring, especially in relation to women and the women's movement.[4] But they have also promised that men could rather easily become "liberated" if they only relinquished their backward attitudes. These books have tended to ignore the difficulty of achieving such change as well as the pain and confusion involved in major shifts in one's life.

Still others have counseled men to reassert their claims to "patriarchy" and masculine dominance, claims supposedly based on biological necessity.[5] I do not share the fear that current changes in the roles of men and women ultimately violate genetic or biological laws (indeed, if such "laws" were so deep-seated, we would be *unable* to violate them at all), nor do I feel that recent alterations in male thought and action are necessarily harmful. Such books largely disregard the fact that relations between men and women have not been the same at all times and places—that human beings have the unique ability to alter their environment to fit their current needs. "Patriarchy" and male dominance, in fact, have differed at various times and in various settings. We are not condemned to repeat a past that we never made.

Early in my study of male experience and the dilemmas involved in change, I found it important to understand how we learned to become men. Expectations about proper male (and female) behavior grow from cultural and social conditions, and our expectations change with changes in those conditions.[6] We shall thus look first at the ways in which today's men grew up and at how traditional ideas about masculinity were transmitted by fathers and male friends. We shall then look at how these ideas affected our views of woman and at how we also learned from the example of our mothers and first girlfriends. The women's movement of the past decade has perhaps done more than anything else to change the lives of men, and we shall discuss both the impact of that movement and of individual women on adult male experience. In addition, we shall investigate the effects of divorce and remarriage—a situation increasingly common in present-day life.

Next we investigate the place of work in contemporary male experience. Work traditionally has provided a way for men to identify themselves in the world, and we shall ask whether this is still true. We shall also be concerned with the ways in which men have learned to share dual-career family patterns and the feelings they have about those arrangements. The final sections of this book discuss the completion of a cycle in the lives of men, as we consider recent alterations in the process of fatherhood. What sort of lessons do men now transmit to children, and what do our children learn about their fathers? We shall see that in some ways the men in this book continue to follow the models of their own fathers, but that they have significantly broken from many of those patterns, as well. We conclude with an attempt to evaluate the gains and losses which recent change has brought to the lives of men, and we look at the question of whether we are presently witnessing the emergence of a new kind of masculinity, a masculinity generated more by our current experience than by our past training.

"There are lots of ways to be a man today," a young advertising executive tells me. "I feel new demands in my life, but these don't simply replace the old demands. I still fulfill the traditional role of the income earner, but I also assume responsibility for cooking, cleaning the house, and taking care of children. . . . The old expectations are still there and new ones have been added. I suspect that other men feel divided in this way, too." This man is right in thinking that his sense of strain and ambivalence has begun to affect many other men. Such strain is the price that we pay for change in our lives, but as we shall see, the divided feelings of this man and others are not entirely negative. Recent male experience asks us to think seriously about the sources of transition in contemporary life, and it makes us realize that there is no easy-to-achieve male or female "liberation." Besides speaking of new opportunities, we must speak, as well, about the difficult and complex struggles which are part of social and personal change.

Notes

1. I have chosen to concentrate on heterosexual men and to speak of men in the social "mainstream." Recently, studies of homosexual attitudes and modes of life have appeared (see, for example C.A. Tripp, *The Homosexual Matrix* (New York: Mc-Graw-Hill, 1975), and Seymour Kleinberg, *Alienated Affections: Being Gay in America* (New York: St. Martin's Press, 1981). I have not, however, been interested in adding to this literature, but in discovering where necessary how the loosening restrictions on "gay" behavior might have influenced heterosexual men.
2. Daniel J. Levinson, *et al., The Seasons of a Man's Life* (New York: Knopf, 1978), p. 41.
3. George Vaillant, *Adaptation to Life* (Boston: Little, Brown and Co., 1977), pp. 372–73.
4. See Marc Feigen Fasteau, *The Male Machine* (New York: McGraw-Hill, 1974); Jack Nichols, *Men's Liberation* (New York: Penguin, 1974); Warren Farrell, *The Liberated Man* (New York: Random House, 1975); Andrew Tolson, *The Limits of Masculinity* (London: Tavistock, 1977).
5. See Lionel Tiger, *Men in Groups* (Random House, 1969); George Gilder, *Sexual Suicide* (New York: Bantam, 1975) and *Wealth and Poverty* (New York: Basic Books, 1980); Steven Goldberg, *The Inevitability of Patriarchy* (New York: Morrow, 1975); Natalie Gittelson, *Dominus: A Woman Looks at Men's Lives* (New York: Harcourt Brace Jovanovich, 1978).
6. See Donald H. Bell, "Up From Patriarchy: The Male Role in Historical Perspective," in Robert A. Lewis, ed., *Men in Difficult Times: Masculinity Today and Tomorrow* (Englewood Cliffs, N.J.: Prentice-Hall, 1981), pp. 306–23. Joseph H. Pleck, *The Myth of Masculinity* (Cambridge, Massachusetts: MIT Press, 1981), pp. 134, 152–53.

CHAPTER 1

Sons and Fathers

You asked me recently why I maintain that I am afraid of you. As usual, I was unable to think of any answer to your question, partly for the very reason that I am afraid of you, and partly because an explanation of the grounds for this fear would mean going into far more details than I could even approximately keep in mind while talking. And if I now try to give you an answer in writing, it will still be very incomplete, because even in writing, this fear and its consequences hamper me in relation to you and because the magnitude of the subject goes far beyond the scope of my memory and power of reasoning.

—Franz Kafka, *Letter to His Father*

[*The*] *relationship between father and son is one of the toughest things in the world to break down. It seems so natural and it is natural—in fact, it's inevitable—but it separates as much as it joins.*

—William Carlos Williams,
The Selected Letters of William Carlos Williams

Fathers create problems for their sons, and sons for their fathers. It is difficult for us to see the relationship in any but the most prejudiced light. Just as Kafka's vision of his father remained beclouded by fear and confusion, so our feelings about our fathers are the source of much of the division we feel as adult men. Our fathers provide our first model of manhood, and that model survives, embedded deep in our minds and our souls. Many of our fathers taught us how to be competent males—strong, dominant, good at performance, and at "taking care of business." We learned from them how—and how not to—express feelings and emotions, and perhaps, above all, we learned how we should behave with the women in our lives.

And yet the lessons of our fathers are not written in stone, never to be eroded by the passage of time. Our fathers did not prepare us for the altered circumstances of the present, nor for the changing expectations that women have of men and that men have of themselves. Men today seem to feel divided and ambivalent about the legacy of their fathers. In one sense, the conflict between fathers and sons is as old as human life. Although Freud and his followers helped us to understand the conflict, it existed before Hamlet could not find the will to avenge his father's ghost, even before Absalom defied the biblical king, David. In some fundamental manner we are condemned to feel divided and uncertain about our fathers. We are condemned to compete with them, to oppose them, and to seek to replace them.

These perpetual struggles of fathers and sons have now been joined by difficulties of another sort which have arisen from the specific circumstances of the last several decades. In a world which is changing rapidly and in which the expectations of men and women have dramatically shifted, the lessons our fathers taught us and the models of masculinity that they provided are often unacceptable. They conflict directly with new images of masculinity and feminity, with changing sex roles, and with emerging views of a man's place in the world.

We need to discover that winning our manhood is up to us alone; and it may be necessary in the process to reshape and redefine our traditional values. The contemporary women's movement has helped to free women from reproducing their own mother's lives; we men also must learn that we need not follow our fathers' paths. Instead, we now face the need to choose a road for ourselves.

In my own life I came early to an awareness of conflict with my father, conflict which was of a rather traditional nature and which was embedded in childhood experience. I still remember how my father climbed the stairs to our second floor apartment that day when he came home from the Navy and the Pacific war. He was still dressed in his uniform, and I could see the cap on his head as it bobbed up and down while he ascended the landing on which my mother and I stood. By this time I was almost three years old, and I vaguely knew what a "father" was, although I did not connect my ideas about fathers with this large man who had just come home. He had been part of my life for at least my first year until he had gone away to the war, although I remember nothing of him during that early and crucial time. As far as I know, my mother cared for me mostly by herself while I was an infant (as was expected in those days), and although there are early photographs of my father holding me up lovingly for the camera, I guess that he rarely changed my diaper or worried much about feeding times.

Once he was home from overseas, my father and I entered into an abiding struggle. He had spent two years of his middle-twenties away from his wife and family. During that time my mother had in some ways substituted me for him in her affections. Moreover, my father's parents lived in the apartment directly below ours, and my father saw that during the time he was away, I had received the daily love and concern not only of my mother, but of his mother and father as well. He was now determined to put an end to what he saw as the "spoiling" of his son. He was determined to begin to make me into a real man.

Today, of course, there is a large body of psychological theory which explains the sort of struggle my father and I experienced, theory based for the most part on Freudian understandings of Oedipal conflict and on more recent refinements of Freud's insights.[1] Directly after World War II, however, such perceptions were not widely understood outside professional circles, and even if my parents had possessed such knowledge, I doubt if theory alone could have helped much to relieve the immediate conflict between my father and myself, or the many similar conflicts of other returning fathers and their young children.[2]

In looking back, my father emerges as the more strongly etched of my two parents, and what I remember most clearly are the difficult times: the harsh words, the spankings, the physical or emotional distance. But as psychoanalyst D. W. Winnicott points out, a child is aware mainly of the disruption of parental care; it takes for granted the continuity of such care, since this nurturing tends to fulfill the child's deepest expectations. My father, it should be noted, has a very different memory of this time. "Your younger brother, Greg," he says, "was the one who usually asked for it. I can't remember actually raising my hand to you more than a couple of times. Greg, by comparison, would act up every few months, and he would almost beg for a spanking by taunting me and refusing to listen. When the spankings came he would almost never cry but would challenge me to do worse. Although I loved him very much, I sometimes didn't know what to do with that kid." Between fathers and sons—as the novelist Turgenev pointed out long ago—truth seems often to serve its own reality.

I remember good times, too, the times when I wanted to be just like my father. There was the day when he first tried to teach me to play baseball at a park a few miles from our house. I listened carefully, trying to please him by learning the complicated and seemingly crazy rules, but when he told me to "run home" after making a hit, I began to cry with frustration and dread, for how was a four-year-old to find his way back to his house across a forest of busy streets? My father laughed and told me that he'd never make me do such a thing. I might be old enough to learn baseball with him, but I was still a little boy, and I could be sure that he would take care of me. I remember, too, the outings to Bear Mountain or to Palisades Interstate Park for picnics and the time when I visited him at his workshop (in those days he still worked in the skilled embroidery trades with his own father). There is a photograph of us shovelling snow from the driveway and building a snowman during the great blizzard of 1946. I remember also his later business success and how proud I was that he eventually landed an executive job with a major movie studio. In grade school I went around telling kids whose fathers were milkmen and insurance brokers that my father actually worked in the movies: holiest of holies, a wonderful and heavenly dispensation which had miraculously touched my family and myself.

Mostly, however, my father seemed to me a figure of fear and of distance. The war had deprived him of his place of dominance within the household and his claim to my mother's time and love. In his absence I had seemingly replaced him. No doubt I was a spoiled and self-centered kid, wanting exclusive access to my mother's affection. When he returned I was forced to share my mother with him, and since my mother clearly loved him, I found that I would possibly have to become like him, but I continued to hate him as well.

Much psychological theory is concerned with demonstrating that our strongest and most fundamental relationship is with our mothers.[3] Still, it is clear that in many ways our relationship with our fathers has an equal weight in our lives, even if our feelings about him are of a different order and the ambivalence that we eventually confront is of a different kind.[4] As children we relied on our mothers for love and affection, and we harbored secret wishes for union with them, even while we struggled to deny those wishes. We sought to emulate our fathers, however, and attempted in such a way to gain both their approval and our mother's love. We also competed with our fathers to be "real men," to show our toughness and masculinity and thus to win our own place in the world.

To such a complex set of feelings was added still another circumstance. Since our fathers did not generally take a very strong part in child rearing, we tend to be more separate from them than from our mothers. Perhaps somewhat ironically, this helps many of us to see our fathers more clearly and to call up our feelings about them—our admiration and our anger—more easily.

Of course, the traditional reluctance of fathers to share in the sweat and difficulty of child care had many negative results. It helped to estrange us from our fathers (even while we might also identify with them), and it put an undue burden upon women as mothers and nurturers. Yet, for me and for many of the men with whom I have spoken, our relationship with our fathers—what we learned and did not learn from them, how we consciously and unconsciously modelled ourselves after them (and of course, how our fathers, themselves, got their own models and sense of masculinity)—has been of central importance in our lives. Indeed, even a father's death does not reduce his centrality, as many of the men with whom I have spoken have noted. "My father might now be dead," one of them told me, "but he's sure not forgotten. I carry him around with me, always."[5]

Our feelings about our fathers' examples have also been confronted by a recent reality: the expectations which we now meet in the world are of a different sort than those of the past. In addition to being tough and competent males, we are now expected to be nurturers and comforters, as well. No past models now suffice, neither that of the strong and "supermasculine" father, nor even that of a father who might have displayed his softer side and whom we and the world might have considered weak. Many of the men I have spoken with note that they are suspended between the lessons they learned from their fathers and what they have had to learn for themselves. They have not completely traded one model for another but have attempted with varying success to find the way between contradictory messages about what it means to be a man. This is especially true—as we shall see—when they speak about some of the major sources of their self-definition as men: about a sense of male competence, about how we show our feelings and emotions, and, of course, about sex.

"I still have lots of stereotypes from my father," Sam Doucet, a psychotherapist in his mid-thirties, tells me. Sam is a huge, imposing man but is also amazingly gentle and softspoken, and he has many insights about his relationship with his father:

> I still very much hold on to some of his ideas about being strong and potent, and these feelings used to scare me when I was younger, because I felt that I could never fill those images of masculinity. In some ways I still feel that I want to be king of my castle, just like him, and my wife and I joke about that a lot. It's also been important to me to earn more money than she does, even though she's a professional, too, and I feel sometimes that I still want to hold on to stereotypes about women that I got from my father, that basically women are emotional and are nincompoops. . . . You know, I try to filter out these attitudes or make light of them, but they're still buried deep inside.

And another man, a professional economist, has this to say:

> I know that the traditional image of masculinity that I carry around comes from my father. He taught me that men provide for their families and don't show feeling. He was very traditional in this way, but he isn't a macho type—swaggering and tough-acting. He was just competent and reserved. Although I want to be able to show more feeling than he does, I haven't really repudiated all of him. I like his sense of competence, and it's important to me to still be like him in some ways.

The conflict runs deep between accepting a father's example about male competence while rejecting specific aspects of that example. In fact, the theme of competence—of an ability to take care of things and to act well—emerges constantly as men discuss their fathers and seems also a kind of lightning rod for our ambivalent feelings. Most of the men with whom I have spoken come from middle-class backgrounds. Their fathers were for the most part professionals or businessmen, and these fathers seem (in the eyes of their sons, at least) to have applied their sense of mastery at home as well as at work. Such fathers were mainly winners in American life, and their sons today continue to admire their ability to get things done.

"My father is sort of low-keyed," one man told me. "He is self-assured, able, and very competent." This man, whom I'll call Ted Morgan, is fast approaching thirty and is a former academic who today runs a small construction business. "What I mainly got from my father," Ted says, "is an outrageous sense of self-confidence. He wasn't tub-thumping or heavy handed about it, but he could do lots of things well. As a kid I remember him showing me how to put a disposal in the sink, or how to build a basketball backboard, and this sort of thing applies in my profession now, because he really helped to demystify the physical world for me and to teach me how to work." This father also gave his son lessons in less overt ways:

> He was a lawyer and a state legislator, and he gave me the ability, I think, to understand issues and to discuss them intelligently. Even though he was involved in public life we didn't talk much politics or law around the dinner table. But I would sometimes go down to the state capital when the legislature was in session, and I would attend committee meetings with him. I remember being impressed with my father's poise and how he could cut through the bullshit of legislative rigamorole. I remember that he once criticized a whole committee of tax experts for their elaborate plans, and he claimed that he had written a better tax package at his kitchen table a few years before. From this I think I began to get some of my suspicion of complex expert formulas.

Not many men, however, have actually had the chance to see their fathers at their jobs. For most of us, our fathers' place of work was a shadowy realm to which they hurried on early morning commuter trains and from which they returned tired out in the evenings. Our sense of our fathers' competence most often arose from how they acted at home and in the tasks that they did around the house. Often, men speak of the ways that their fathers handled tools and of their abilities in building and construction. "I learned that woodworking was something that one could do by watching him build and exercise his skills," one man tells me, while another says, "My father didn't do carpentry or things like that too often, but he was very competent when he did. He built cabinets in our kitchen, for example. For some reason, however, I really didn't take after him in those ways much. I'm not skillful in working with my hands, and I'm not sure why. I didn't just reject his values, but I was very much into athletics, an interest I also got from him." Another man, James, a hospital administrator, notes:

> Competence implies a set of norms which are very hard to pin down. In social situations my father holds back and doesn't interact too much, so in that way I wouldn't call him very competent. But he's a very creative man, one of the finest cabinetmakers I've ever known. He's a wonderful artist, and from what I understand, he's good at his professional job. Also, for as long as I can remember, he did the shopping for the family, and every Friday afternoon he brought bags of groceries home from the local market. So if you consider those things, then I guess that he was a very competent individual.

Some of our fathers communicated in other and more "expressive" ways, as well. After telling me about his father's competence in woodworking and in handling tools, psychologist Sam Doucet also told me, "My father sang and made music, too, and he performed in choirs in both churches and synagogues—it didn't really matter where—and he taught me how to sing and play the guitar. . . . It was a very rich experience, getting this sense of culture and self-expression through those kinds of things."

My own father, I should note, was accomplished and competent in lots of ways, but much of what he communicated came in an indirect manner. He fulfilled his dreams of becoming a success in business, first with the movie studio and then on his own. I do not, however, have many memories of seeing him in his professional world. Sometimes I have heard his business cronies praise his cleverness, and one has even told me that he is a true genius in his work, but as a child and adolescent what was important to me was to see him in action around the house. At one time he had been a skilled welder, and the Navy taught him to be an electrician. He had learned woodworking and plumbing from his own father. Early every Saturday, it seemed, he would put those skills to use. He would busily work on building a patio, or on adding a room to the house, or on landscaping the garden. It seemed that he could do so many things well, but he was not too ready to share his knowledge about woodworking or construction with his sons. My two brothers and I would often watch from a distance as he moved from one job to another, and I got the feeling that this kind of activity provided him a way of letting off steam after a long week at the office.

This performance, I think, might also have been a kind of wistful elegy for the lost world of skilled craft labor which he had left behind in his climb up the middle-class ladder. Once in awhile, my father would call on my brothers or me for some help, but usually at those times he carefully laid out the ground rules and reserved for himself both the sense of how the overall job was to be done and what tools were needed. I felt that in his eyes my brothers and I were indentured assistants who were there to follow his instructions and who had to do the job his way or not at all. My two younger brothers learned a certain amount of woodworking and craft from him (perhaps by the time they came along he was a bit softer and less hurried). I, by comparison, found myself in retreat from my father's work brigades, and I studiously avoided learning much about carpentry or electrical wiring from his indirect and hasty lessons. Even today, I feel this as a loss and I wonder if I should have made more of an effort as a child or teenager to ask him clearly to teach me the skills that he had at his command.

A sense of a father's competence or incompetence runs as a theme through the lives of men. Even where our fathers clearly lacked mastery, we seek to find ways in which they were skilled and accomplished and in which they can be useful to our own search for ourselves. Jim Cohen, a novelist who has written often about his relationship with his father, told me about his father's lack of business acumen and about how his mother constantly treated the father as a " 'poor *schlimiel*' who made no money and had no courage to change." "My father was a very angry man," Jim relates. "He couldn't control the world and he felt really helpless and sad. He was a big, physically strong guy who felt inadequate mentally, and what he taught me was failure and incompetence. . . . In fact, from the time I was six years old I knew through my mother that I was smarter than my father, this 'poor fool.' "

Not satisfied with that remembrance, Jim in adult life has sought to discover parts of his father that were more positive. "I think today," he says, "that as a salesman my father was not as incompetent as my mother made out. When I went back to where we lived, I found out that he got along well with people, and that his friends really loved him, and that today these friends remember him with real affection. This, I think, is what I get from him," Jim continues, "this sense of a lot of affection with the people you work with and see around you. . . . He was always very tender with me, very affectionate, and very loving. He was constantly touching me and being physical. In fact, I have the same thing with my own kids today, and I get it directly from him. Despite everything, my father had a great deal of love to give."

In creating his father as a kind of fictional character, in reviewing and reliving his father's behavior and failures, this man has rendered his father into a kind of mythological figure. If anything, he shares his own father's sweetness of personality, his father's ability to be physical and expressive, and to be kind with those for whom he cares. In writing about his father and of his father's weaknesses and strengths, Jim has actually made his father an accomplice in his own literary success and an agent of his own personal development.

As adults struggling with the male roles we have been taught to play, we still hold on to what we see as the positive sides of our fathers' example. Our fathers' abilities, their sense of mastery (however broad or limited) anchors us against our drift into the unknown. And yet much of our own ambivalence about change arises from our rejection of many of the lessons which our fathers taught.

"I admire my father's ability," one man tells me, "and I learned from him that it's important to be competent in what you're doing." He pauses to think carefully, and then he adds as an afterthought: "But being competent doesn't really mean having to present yourself in the traditional ways my father did. There are lots of ways to appear to be competent and on top of things that are just modes of acting and that doesn't have anything to do with being good at what you're doing at all." The lessons that our fathers taught us were sometimes confusing and are often not very functional in our own adult lives. At moments, however, they can still be useful and instructive to us. In part, being a male adult today means knowing how to choose between the good lessons and the bad. It also means wanting to be judged by older standards yet wishing, too, to be measured by the new.

Men feel conflict and uneasiness about other paternal legacies. What fathers pass on about the expression of feelings and emotions is one source of ambivalence.

Ted Morgan, for example, tells me that "what I learned from my father, number one, two, and three, was not to be emotionally expressive. My father was fair to me in many ways when I was a kid. We did lots of things together: he coached a Little League team that I was on, for example, but the level of emotional expressiveness was very low."

"In fairness," Ted adds, "that's since changed some. We're more expressive today. We can now hug and kiss when we meet . . . and I think that this change came in both of us independently. I learned from the women I was with that it was O.K. to show feelings, and I guess that as my father grows older his children and his family become more important to him."

Ted Morgan's ability to express feeling and emotion with his father now is similar to what I, myself, have experienced. Many men, however, have not seen such changes in emotional tone. "My father has never shown much affection or feeling," a young East coast attorney tells me:

> People just didn't get mad in the house, and maybe as a result, I have no model for seeing how a person gets angry and for learning that anger

doesn't actually destroy us. . . . I've never seen my father cry, and I've never cried in front of him as an adult. I sense that it would have been terrible if I did. In that way, I'm a lot like my father. I'm careful about showing feeling, and up till now I've only shown emotions from a distance. But showing how I feel is constantly becoming more important for me, and part of me doesn't get satisfied unless I can be honest about expressing how I feel. I now sense that I'm not really getting what I want out of life if I can't express my emotions. So this is more important for me all the time, and it's really an ongoing struggle.

"A lot of things have been expected of men which are really not very nice," another man notes:

For example, since a man was supposedly big and strong, he shouldn't have any emotions or feelings. And since I happen to be tall and strong, this kind of thing seemed to apply to me very much. But whether your feelings get hurt doesn't have to do with how physically big you are. The only way I could handle this contradiction as a kid and an adolescent was to withdraw and to cover up what went on inside. I now know that my father's inability to show his feelings had a lot to do with how I handled this.

It is clear that our fathers sometimes went to rather extraordinary lengths to avoid expressing their own inner worlds. "My father was really a strange guy," a lawyer tells me:

He was totally incapable of showing feelings, and it wasn't even a question of rational choice for him. My mother says that he would show her affection by sometimes doing the housework, since he had more energy than she did, but otherwise, he didn't show anyone a thing. He couldn't even call my mother by her name; he called her 'mother' instead, and when the time came, he called her 'grandma.' She would really plead with him to use her name, but he just couldn't do it. He was just so uptight in his feelings. He was such a tight person that even calling her by her name made him nervous.

Not all fathers were as inexpressive as this, and for the most part we learned from them that there were certain acceptable ways for us to show what went on inside. When I was a child my own father was able to show his anger (or at least it seemed that way to me). We would all often sit impassively together at the dinner table, scene of our main daily contact as a family. It was clear when my father had had a bad day at the office, for then our mostly silent meals might be punctuated by a sharp word from him or by a mordant commentary on our table manners which would set my brothers and me to wolfing down our food, the sooner to be away from that scene of confrontation. I can at this moment feel what it was like to steel myself against this criticism and try to present a cold and invulnerable exterior to him and to the world. In that way I seemed to be like my father, but it is clear now that much of his ability to express certain feelings came from his own father, my grandfather, Dan.

As a young child I would go on long car outings alone with Dan, and I would watch him yell at other drivers, gesticulating in an angry manner. Once, when we came home, I innocently informed my mother that Dan and I had seen a lot of sons-of-bitches that day—the name my grandfather used for most of the other drivers on the road. My father probably learned his ability to express emotion from Dan, but for him it took another form. My father almost never yelled at other drivers, for example, nor did he speak harshly to my mother, as Dan sometimes did to his wife, my grandmother. Legacies are passed across generations much as images are infinitely reflected in opposed sets of mirrors, but we sometimes attach meanings of our own to these intergenerational legacies, keeping those that seem to serve our needs, and rejecting the rest.

In childhood and adolescence I found from both father and grandfather (and from media images of men), that it was acceptable to give vent to frustration and anger. This could be done, however, only at certain times and in certain ways. In high school I could swagger with my friends and act tough, and I could get into fights to show my manly strength and cool. It was "masculine" to express anger.

I soon learned that one had to be careful about whom one pushed around and when one fought. It was always important to challenge (or to "choose off" as we said in high school) only those who were equal in size and strength—and preferably those who were a bit smaller and weaker. I do not know exactly how I learned this essential lesson of male survival, but there it was: prove yourself in manly combat, but don't blow your cool by losing.

Playing football, too, was an accepted way to let off anger and emotion, and since my father had been a high school football star, it was rather easy for me to adopt the pose of the tough and aggressive male athlete. My body was relatively well developed. I did enjoy sports. If I couldn't compete with the myth of my father as a football standout, I could gain a bit of glory in my own right. Today, I am stunned by photographs of myself as a mean middle-linebacker on my high school team, grimacing for the camera and ready to put the world away with a bone-crushing tackle. A few months ago, I spoke with an attorney who had once been the quarterback of an opposing high school team in my home town. "You were really some crazy fucker," he said. "Do you remember how you tried to fight me at a party, and how you screamed and called me a 'chicken-shit' when I refused to fight you?" I felt myself squirm and blush in shame, and I was glad that we were speaking on the telephone where he couldn't see my face. "Was that really me?" I thought. "Maybe you're mistaken?" And yet I knew that it had indeed been me and that my expression of rage and anger had seemed at the time the most appropriate way (and, in fact, almost the only way) to display my feelings and my masculinity.

Perhaps the only time in those years that I saw my father in relation to an alternative model of masculine behavior was when my friend Peter and I set off for our freshman year in college. Our fathers had agreed to make the drive with us to the university, a distance of nearly five hundred miles. This expedition from home to dormitory was part of the ritual by which fathers sent sons off into the world. Pete's father was a rather prominent psychiatrist, and he was a man capable of showing a wide variety of feelings. All four of us traveled in the antiquated and beat-up Dodge convertible which Pete's dad normally drove to and from his practice. It soon became clear that this would be no ordinary trip. As I remember, my father did much of the driving, while Pete's father sat barechested and flabby in the back seat, sweating and strumming his guitar and crooning "Careless Love" and "Freight-train," as Pete and I chimed in. The more we sang and clowned, the more this seemed to upset my father. He stepped down on the accelerator, in the hope, I think, of ending this ordeal as quickly as possible and ridding himself of the unseemly Doctor. Finally, a highway patrol officer pulled us over for speeding, and from that point on my father said very little. When we reached the university, I could tell that he was more than glad to have the journey over. I knew that he was happy to see me begin college, and he was proud that he could send me there. He had not gone beyond high school, himself, and seeing his eldest son become an undergraduate must have been a great joy for him.

Still, the joy went mostly unexpressed as he hurried away. He had to catch a plane back home, he said, but I suspected that he had hastily made those arrangements to escape the return journey with the mad Doctor.

Some men, however, recall other ways their fathers could express emotions. "My father was a kind and sensitive person, but he was not very open," says a medical doctor, the son of a clergyman:

> He was a loving person and he was genuinely warm to others. This was rooted in his Christian morality which he took to be a requirement and a guide. . . . I saw him cry on a number of occasions when he was sad, and sometimes when I would do something that upset him he would get so exasperated that he would be moved to tears. From him I guess I learned that it was all right for men to cry.
>
> And yet, my father was not a very physical person—about the only physical contact we had was when I was in grade school, and my sister and I would wrestle with him on Friday evenings while my mother made popcorn in the kitchen. And also there was a certain sexual oppressiveness about him. We would never discuss sex when I was growing up; there was a repressive mood about sex in our family which seemed to come from both my father and my mother.

Another man tells me:

> My father was (and is) a very gentle man. In some ways he's very unassertive and this has been a problem for me, since I've had to work hard to learn to assert myself. My father always had a very sensitive and caring relationship with my mother and in some ways he was a more nurturing person than she was. When she died last spring it was a long ordeal. I was with him a lot, and he didn't hold his feelings inside. He cried with me and expressed the whole variety of emotions that people in grief go through.
>
> So you see, my father doesn't have difficulty sharing his sadness. He could always do this, and I'm glad and grateful because it meant that I didn't have to unlearn all kinds of negative patterns that I see other men struggling to unlearn.
>
> Except my father couldn't show anything to do with anger. Both he and my mother came from families which felt that to show anger was beneath one's dignity. This has been a real problem for me and for almost everyone in my family. It was a way that my father and I didn't share at

> all. In adolescence all I could do was to withdraw when I was angry with my parents, since I didn't get much validation for these feelings. Today, in fact, I'm just learning that you can be angry at the people that you love and that it doesn't mean that you hate them. You can be angry and can express your anger, and can still be in control. It's just part of the natural spectrum of human emotions and it is a legitimate feeling. So over the last year, I've been talking with my father and others in my family to see if we can now work out some better ways of dealing with whatever anger we have.

We learned from our fathers that if men could express any feeling at all, it would be confined to a narrow range. Many of us grew up with the notion that a man should not allow the full spectrum of his emotions to break through, and that he could not expose to his sons his anger and sadness, elation and despair, joy and pain. We seemed, above all, to have inherited no vocabulary for showing our inner selves or for shifting from one feeling to another. To be a man meant to conceal the worrisome traces of an inner life, and at most to show one or another prepackaged or habitual reaction to what really went on inside. That was the way of the world, after all, and the legacy of preceding male generations. It is a legacy which men are beginning to renounce for many reasons. Women are insisting that we change and sometimes they show us how. It is also part of the current climate: the lessons of the revolutionary sixties were compounded and freshened during the not-so-static seventies. Living one's life for the moment—"going for the gusto," as the beer ads would have it—has become part of the social framework, and although often derided as symptomatic of a "narcissistic" and self-serving culture, this particular variety of narcissism seems to make some sense. As one man said to me, "I'm not really living and getting what I need out of life if I can't express my emotions. . . . This is more important all the time. . . ." Oddly enough, as we begin to leave the example of our fathers behind, our fathers have, themselves, often begun to change in surprising ways. As we shall see, the men whom we thought to be little more than the stereotypical Archie Bunker or the poker-faced Victorian *paterfamilias* have started to flower on their own.

Another source of ambivalence and divided feelings during childhood and adolescence was our own sexuality. Because of lingering puritanism and possibly because of their own deep-seated feelings of ambivalence, fathers were generally reluctant to discuss sexual matters with their sons, nor did they commonly acknowledge their sons' growth as sexual beings. Men experience very little sexual sharing with their fathers, whatever the prevailing male mythology has to say on the subject. In sexuality, as in so many other areas, fathers provide us a model of male behavior, and yet they impede us from finding new models of our own.

Evidence of this surrounds us, from parental resistance to sex education courses in schools to the cryptic messages about "being good, but being careful," that fathers transmit when teenage sons try to borrow the car for a Saturday night date. It is a problem which even later in life seems to haunt us, and in talking about the ways (or non-ways) that fathers discussed sex and sexuality, men tend to convey a sense of loss and some bitterness. "I got a lot of my sense of myself from my father," one man told me. "He helped me to be comfortable in the physical world and he made me interested in understanding things intellectually, but as far as being a man sexually, the understandings I got from my father didn't have to do with my own maleness. What I mean is that I just didn't get any sexual understanding from him, period. He was really a pretty repressed person."

And another man, a schoolteacher, spoke candidly about the misinformation his father gave him and of his own anger because of this. "Being from a strong Catholic family," he says, "we never talked about sex. The only time my father ever spoke about it when I was a teenager was to ask me if I masturbated and to tell me that it would make me lose control of orgasm, that I might shoot in my pants if I made a habit of playing with myself. This made me really frightened, and later, when I learned it wasn't true, I was really pissed at my father for telling me this kind of lie. It was such incongruous behavior on his part, I felt, because he generally was truthful with me." A bit wistfully he adds, "I guess that talking about sex really did something strange to my father, that in some way it made him not be himself."

At times, men speak with a kind of gallows humor about the ways that their fathers conveyed messages about sex, as if joking will help ease the feeling of loss and the sense of having missed something really important. "Once, my father told me that if there was anything I didn't know, I should feel free to ask," a young medical doctor says. "Naturally, this approach turned me off, and I never was comfortable enough to ask him anything—maybe, in fact, that was what he actually wanted to happen. At Christmas one year, my parents actually put my younger sister up to giving me a book about sex. She gave me the book with a nice, unknowing smile, and my parents got a big kick out of it. They did this as a joke, and to relieve the tension that they probably felt about being direct. We all had a big laugh about it, as I remember."

"He wasn't a good warm father in teaching me how to shave, or to go out with women, or about sex," a fortyish newspaper reporter says with a reflective smile. "In fact, he was horrible about it. He tried to fill me in about the birds and bees, but he was really so clumsy. He's a wonderfully decent man, but he's a very shy person, and discussing women and sex really had him all tied up. He actually didn't even know how to start or what words to use."

The kinds of lessons fathers often conveyed came less from what they actually said than from messages they transmitted through their behavior. Edward, a financial analyst, notes that he probably got a sense from his father of the need to be in control with women and especially to be in control while making love. "My father is not dynamically assertive," Edward says, "and he's not aggressive about taking control. He merely implies that 'since I'm a man, you should let me be in charge,' and this is just the way I am with women, myself. It's as if his way of withdrawing from contact with others had become a model for me in handling threatening feelings, and especially feelings about sexuality and about the intimacy that might be involved in sex."

I remember that when I was a boy and an adolescent, I, too, got very mixed messages from my father (and also, my mother) about sex. Like many men, I cannot recall having spoken about such matters at home, nor did my father make overtures to fill me in on what young males should know and what I needed to be careful about. When it was time to deal with such things, it was my mother who gave me a book on the forbidden subject—as I remember it was entitled something like *What Every Teenage Boy Needs to Know About Sex*. As with most other men (and women, too), who experienced such an approach to parental sex education, I did not learn much from the well-intentioned book. From age twelve or so I had learned a lot through the mutual fumblings and feelings which happened with girlfriends at junior high school make-out parties. That, and the chatter, bravado, and experimentation of my male schoolmates was my real introduction to the world of sex. Part of the legacy which my generation carries around, I've discovered, is its instant recall of the rock and roll songs which were played at those eighth grade parties. Another part of our legacy is the way we were initiated into sex: not by parents, but by peers; not with any sense of clarity and rational care, but with a slipshod and halting introduction to the holy mystery.

The only real messages my father conveyed, I think, were mostly negative ones, and these set me wondering at how something which felt so good (my sexual feelings and fantasies) could supposedly be so bad. On the eve of my teenage years, I began to paste pictures all over my room of scantily clad women clipped from the pages of *Argosy* magazine and *Esquire*. (In those days *Playboy* was still too difficult for a twelve-year-old to buy, and I am not really sure how I got copies of the magazines from which I cut my pinup beauties—I probably bought them under the counter from unscrupulous newsdealers, or I shoplifted them, driven to this act of desperation by sexual longings which seemed unrelenting, but which I scarcely understood.)

This went on for a few months, for my room was over the garage, and my parents rarely set foot in my slovenly lair. One day, however, my father got wind of what was occurring, and he tore from the walls all of my carefully culled pinup women. As he cut the pictures to shreds, I vainly attempted to explain that this excursion into early teenage experimentation was somehow an innocent project I had devised to decorate my rather shabby quarters. Needless to say, the nudes never returned to my walls. I was driven underground, and I had to content myself with flipping through the magazines which I now hid behind the bookshelves and which I brought out only in the dead of night.

The next year I foolishly began to read Erskine Caldwell's *God's Little Acre* as part of a ninth grade English class project, and I was dumbfounded when my parents were called to have a conference with my teacher about my taste in reading matter. I had seen reference to the Caldwell book while reading *Battle Cry* or some other novel of military bravery. The book sounded interesting (probably because it dealt with sex), and so I got a copy by one of my usual methods. I innocently thought that printed literature fundamentally differed from pinup art and was thus a relatively safe way to deceive my parents. I found that I was wrong, and as in the case of my pictures, my father confiscated Caldwell's genre tale of Southern promiscuity (most of which I did not understand, anyway), and he threatened to monitor my reading habits in the future (a threat which, in fact, he never carried out, but which once again drove me to underground expedients).

The only other times I can recall dealings with my father over sexual matters occurred much later, in high school and in college. In a way, my father was not directly involved in these episodes at all, but merely appeared as the wrathful internal father which I had by now firmly made part of myself. Once, after having some sort of genital contact as a high school sophomore (I do not think I actually had intercourse), I developed what I thought was a suspicious rash in my pubic area, and I immediately began to fear the worst: it was certainly V.D., and even more seriously, my father would surely have to be told what I'd been doing. A friend soon fixed me up, however, with a sympathetic doctor. (I surmised that this doctor's willingness to deal with minors and not to inform parents was a sign of medical incompetence.) I found to my great relief that I did not have a communicable social disease. The doctor took one look at my penis and at the slight redness which had so bedeviled me, and he told me to wash better after football practice and to go easy on the masturbation, and that was that.

Then, in college, I was driven to distraction by the fear that I had made my girlfriend pregnant one night during a drunken party. The fear, in fact, was not at all for her welfare or for the predicament that we might both be in together. It was rather a fear of discovery by my father (as well as self-punishment by the internalized father I had constructed). How, I pondered, was I to ask my father for $500—the going price of a Tijuana abortion? That would mean telling him what I'd actually been doing and that I'd not been diligently striving to vindicate his hopes for me or appreciating the sacrifices he had made. Fearing that I had blown all my chances for a normal and successful life, I spent the better part of the next month in bed at my fraternity house, paralyzed with anxiety that he would discover that I was still the same teenage sex maniac whose pinups he had ripped from the wall. I had not taken care of myself (although he had never given me any direction on how to do so), and so ended up in a real jam. Finally, Peggy Sue announced that she'd gotten her period, and the crisis was at an end. (I still think, in fact, that she might have actually arranged for her own abortion, deciding out of womanly self-confidence and empathy not to tell me while she carried out her plans alone.) I vowed not to have sex for a while (it was dangerous, I found), and if I ever did it again, to be stone sober and to use a fresh prophylactic instead of the age-old denizen of my wallet which had almost predictably broken with Peggy Sue and I began our fun.

In talking with my own son about sex, I think I have been for the most part open and direct and that I have started to break with a traditional pattern as many other contemporary fathers also have. At about age nine, Jacob implied that he had learned nearly all there was to know from his friends and from television (kids are more precocious today—a gain in some ways, a real loss in others). Sara, my present wife, insisted that now was the time to talk openly with him, and when I did, I found that he did not know much at all. I was surprised at my initial resistance to discuss sex with him and at the excuses that I gave about a nine-year-old being too young to understand such matters. Perhaps I really was obeying some ingrained parental message about fathers not speaking with children about sexuality. Finally, I plucked up my courage, and fortified with intellectual arguments about the importance of the new openness between fathers and sons, I spoke with him one afternoon as we were virtual captives on a drive to the airport where he was to fly back to his mother. As I said, he did not know very much, and initially he could not believe my explanations about the purpose of menstruation or about how people actually had intercourse ("C'mon, they don't really do it that way . . . ?"). I left out some of the finer details for future sex talks, but I was amazed to discover that both my ex-wife and her new husband, as well as Sara, herself, were waiting for me as a father to talk with this precocious child. This message came through only haltingly, however, and it was as if there was an enormous distance between my intellectual understanding of the need for a new road in the relationship between fathers and sons, and my actual capabilities to be as open as I would like to be. In any event, Jake has now had his sex talk (and since then, one or two more), and he and I have made a beginning. Old messages are deeply ingrained, and it takes more than just good intentions and promises to oneself to bring about change.

If physical closeness and frankness about sex has been mostly off limits to fathers and sons, the sharing of sports and athletics seems somehow a compensation in our society. In his book, *Jock Culture,* Neil Isaacs notes that, "Sports has entered the fabric and structure of our whole way of life. Sports is a constant, a model, a value system. It is our strength and our weakness, our redeemer and destroyer. . . . Intellectually and philosophically, emotionally and psychologically, sexually and physically, sports governs our lives."[6] Sports, in brief, provide a metaphor for American life and afford a way for fathers to introduce sons to the meanings and expectations, the punishments and rewards of our culture.

Although in adolescence I was never conscious of how important my father's interest in sports was to me, I continually attempted to impress him with my abilities on the baseball diamond or the football field. I was enormously proud when, shortly after my ninth birthday, I was chosen to be on a Little League team with the bigger boys in town, because I knew that this would be a way to show my father how manly and competent I had become. I have since learned that many contemporaries had similar experiences, and far more men than I thought possible had fathers who actually coached their Little League teams, mostly out of a sense that this was part of the dues which a "good father" had to pay. Instead of bringing them closer to their sons, however, such a tactic only rendered these fathers more imposing as authority figures, and it often left the sons confused and embarrassed about being shown excessive parental favoritism or being given excessive parental blame.

Rooting vicariously for professional teams also helped make for contact between fathers and sons. This kind of sports allegiance seems to run in families, and since in my own case, my fathers and uncles followed the Brooklyn Dodgers with religious zeal (while a single eccentric uncle held out desperately for Willie Mays and the Giants), my brothers and I found ourselves fervent Dodger fans, as well. This family loyalty continued even after the Brooklynites transplanted themselves to Los Angeles, an event which occurred in the very same year that our own family moved from the East to Southern California. We happily maintained our allegiance to the Dodgers in a new and strangely exotic setting. To this day, in fact, the Dodgers still provide my father, my brothers, and me with an inevitable topic of conversation, and I often find myself compelled to turn first to the morning sports page (as does my father) to check on the previous day's doings in Chavez ravine.

Violent contact sports help to build traditional male "character" in this society, and fathers have often promoted such experience for their sons. Just as often—and sometimes secretly—sons have reacted against this pressure to perform on the field of combat. "My father got me boxing gloves when I was in junior high," one man says, "and I remember learning to box with my friends. . . . I just couldn't seem to deal with it, though. I didn't want to hit anyone or to be hit, and it was hard to avoid bad feelings when we were supposed to be having these friendly fights." Another man tells me of the pressure that he felt from his father's demand that he excel in sports (and in other ways, as well): "It's only now, when I'm an adult," he says, "that I can finally get back to just liking to play baseball or to throw a frisbee around without feeling the sense of having to perform or to win at all costs that my father emphasized."

I do not have a clear sense of how I learned to follow in my father's athletic footsteps. Years after I had played football in high school (where I was a lineman—as my father had been), and after boxing on my college team as a light-heavyweight (the same weight division in which my father had competed in the Navy), I still cannot clearly locate the parental messages which helped me to do these things. Such messages were not very overt, and at times my parents even showed some disapproval of the contact sports which I had chosen, but I know that in order to become a man—and even ironically to free myself from my father's influence—I needed to pass through some of the same physical challenges and to reach some of the same levels of bodily mastery. Even though I discovered, as well, that I did not particularly like to hit or to be hit, I persisted, and I still have a sharply etched remembrance of how punches look as they float upward toward one's face, and of how they explode with a thud on one's gloves, or headgear, or nose, and of how one often sees a flash of light on impact when making a hard tackle, and of how that tackle jolts one's body from helmet through spine. I think that at a certain point I needed to learn these things and to see if I could enter this world of male aggression as my father had done, and to reproduce in myself the physical experience and achievements of his own life.

Often I fear that I have begun to transmit some of the same messages to my own son. Although I carefully warn Jake about the dangers of playing football, and although I habitually show him the scar which lines my shoulder from a football-induced operation, I still laud him for his prowess on his playground touch football team, or for a sensational catch that he makes when we throw the ball around. Both Jake and I remain glued to the TV tube, comparing notes on an Earl Campbell run, or dissecting a Terry Bradshaw pass, or minutely discussing the defensive coverage of the Dallas secondary and the hitting abilities of the L.A. linebackers. When we go out to the park to run pass patterns, I play the wily quarterback, he the shifty receiver. At such times I am enchanted by our closeness and camaraderie (a closeness which we share in many other ways), but I am also appalled by the suspicion that I have helped create a monster. "No, stop!" I want to shout. "This is all wrong. I'm going to do it differently. Things aren't the same; I'm not a traditional kind of father. Look, we can hold each other, we can play chess or bake bread together, we can share intimate secrets. We don't need to rely on football or boxing, or on violence." And yet, we do share the experience of violent sports, and in the face of my deepest resolve, I feel myself inevitably part of a process which transmits and reproduces a traditional malehood.

There is one consolation in all of this: I am aware of what my messages might mean to my son, and I can talk with him about such meanings. Our own fathers, in contrast, did not for the most part have that option. Raised in a more traditional world, they survived mainly by reproducing the messages and the masculinity of the past.

Our fathers did not prepare us for the altered circumstances of the present, nor could we have expected them to do so. In a rapidly changing world we are finally left with the formidable and scary task of creating ourselves as men: learning how to show the full range of our feelings—our anger, love, sadness, elation, despair, and joy; learning how to change our behavior when past behavior no longer suffices; and learning how to transmit our new sense of manhood to our children. If the women's movement has enabled women to be more than just the sum of their own mothers' experience, men no longer need merely reproduce that of their fathers. This is a heady and frightening discovery, and its fearsomeness bears in on me every time my wife leaves in the morning to earn the major portion of our family bread, or even as I wash the dishes, or do the laundry, or when I cry, or try to express my joy, or love, or grief. I realize that I am beginning to become a new kind of man, one who can follow few of the traditional guideposts—a man who has mainly the experience of other contemporary men and women to rely upon for support and sustenance.

As men today, we are in conflict with the lessons our fathers taught us. We loved and respected our fathers, but we also hated them and wanted to replace them. They loved us and wanted us to be like them (or even better), but often they had difficulty in showing this love, and they tended to treat us as rivals. They taught us that men were controlled and competent, whether in work or in personal life. They showed us that a man should not express much emotion and that overt expressiveness was weak and feminine. A real man could argue or be angry, but he could not show fear, and he could not weep. Finally, our fathers served as models for our sexual feelings and actions. They probably wanted us to be sexually successful males, but they did not often talk with us about sex, nor did they want us to be sexual too early. More importantly, they helped to inculcate the message that the right kind of male sexuality was dominant and rather aggressive. One could presumably talk lovingly to a woman, but one avoided expressing too much tenderness or affection for fear of becoming submissive. Maleness was defined in terms of strength and competence, whether in work, in sexual relationships, or in sports. Today such messages—transmitted by fathers from their *own* store of social learning—no longer serve very well. It has become clear to many contemporary men that life is not merely an athletic contest to be won at all costs and that women are not rivals to be overcome. It is all right to cry, and it is important to seek equality with our female counterparts—whether lovers, wives, co-workers, or friends. Such new lessons come at a cost, however, and we are faced with finding ways to transcend our fathers' legacy while choosing to keep the best of that legacy, as well.

POSTSCRIPT

One oddity of living in a time of great change is that such change is not limited to certain parts of our lives but instead occurs in unlikely as well as expected places. It has been the experience of many of the men I have interviewed (as it has been my own experience) that once we have described how our fathers acted in the past, we must also describe how they presently act. A paradox enters here, for many of our fathers have changed greatly over the last several years (while our perceptions of them have altered, as well). Numerous men with whom I have spoken confide that their fathers are now more caring and expressive, less aggressive and driven than they were only a few years ago. One man tells me, for example, that "change has come from both of us. We're both more expressive now. We hug and kiss when we see each other, and we've both learned that it's O.K. to do this," and another man says:

> It feels very nice with my father now. I've gone through a lot in terms of being critical of him, but in the last two or three years I've become less aware of him as a father and more aware of a man who's experienced a lot of ups and downs. . . . We've learned to be more direct with each other, and now he can come to visit, and we can share my house and

> the new things in my life and more family feeling, as well. . . . I see him much less as a big daddy or the stern, strong, invulnerable man, and I now see mostly his gentleness and his warmth which might always have been there, along with a certain reserve which he always used to hide his sensitive feelings.

"We've both changed," this man concludes. "I've become more responsible for calling out his feelings, and he finds it easier to show his inner self to me."

In the same way, James, the hospital administrator, tells me, "My father has finally stopped trying to pretend to be something that he's not. He's no longer concerned with being a 'man' in the eyes of society, and he's more concerned with just being himself. . . . Today he'll think nothing of putting on an apron to cook with my mother, and he'll make things on the sewing machine. He was always creative, but he's now allowing that creativity to come through, and he's more able to express what might seem the feminine parts of his personality."

My own father, I should note, has changed in some of these ways, as well. Today, in his early sixties, he is open and generous and more warm than I ever remember him being. He can laugh at himself and at the sillier ways of the world. He can allow himself to be much more supportive of my brothers and me. He recently gave strong backing, for example, to the plans of one of us to move to a new city (much to our surprise, for we had always perceived him as the voice of caution and "reason"), and he has shared with me his experience of hard moments and one-time unemployment in a loving and supportive way. "Once, more than ten years ago," he told me, "I waited on the unemployment lines in Hollywood. I was there with some of the top stars and actors in the business who were temporarily between jobs. These things pass. Go with the experience of your own temporary unemployment, and learn from it. And laugh, if you can." This lesson paid off for him, it seems. Today, he feels successful and secure in his business and in his world. He is a man with much tenderness, love, and sensitivity. Over the past few years he has begun to share this with others and to acknowledge it in himself.

Our perception of change in our fathers, however, is partly the result of changes in our own observing lens: the men in their thirties and forties with whom I have spoken have entered a more mature period of their own development, and they can now see their fathers in a less judgmental light. They are no longer closely tied to former images of their fathers and to earlier needs to follow in their own fathers' path.

Such changes have also taken place in an independent way and can be attributed less to our own observation than to the stages of the life cycle into which these fathers have embarked. Many of them are now living through their sixties and seventies, a stage which psychologist Erik Erikson has described as being basically concerned with the polarity of "integrity versus despair"—that is, with finding a mode of living which summarizes the meaning of one's contribution to life in the face of old age and impending death. In the words of researcher Joseph Levinson, who has investigated the stages of adult development, this period late in life can afford an opportunity for forming, "a broader perspective . . . and more profound [recognition] of our human contradictions, creativity, and destructiveness. . . . It means that [a man] becomes less interested in obtaining the rewards offered by society, and more interested in utilizing his own inner resources. The voices within the self become, as it were, more audible and more worthy of his attention."[7] I think this is a fine description of the behavior and the changes experienced by the fathers of many of the men in this book.

Such changes, however, have still another source: the social turmoil of the 1960s and 1970s and the women's movement itself. If changes in the role and situation of the women who have been in the forefront of that movement have had great impact on younger men, they have a pronounced effect on older men as well. "Maybe it's the women's movement, maybe it's that he's now sixty-four," one man said about his father, "but he's less tight now than he ever was, and he can express his inner feelings in more direct ways." Many of these older men continue to grouse about the changes and the upset which feminism has produced (my father, for example, insists on referring to my wife as "Mrs. Bell," although he knows that she specifically decided not to change her name when we were married), but they have benefited from the feminist movement in ways which they might not fully understand. They no longer must serve as traditional models for a fading and constricted masculinity, and they are freer than ever before to become who they might really wish to be.

Notes

1. See, for example, Nancy Chodorow, *The Reproduction of Mothering* (Berkeley and Los Angeles: University of California Press, 1978); Dorothy Dinnerstein, *The Mermaid and the Minotaur* (New York: Harper and Row, 1976); David B. Lynn, *The Father: His Role in Child Development* (Monterey, California: Brooks/Cole, 1974).

2. See L.M. Stolz, *et al.*, *Father Relations of War-Born Children* (Stanford, California: Stanford University Press, 1975); H.B. Biller, *Parental Deprivation* (Lexington, Massachusetts: D.C. Heath and Co., 1974).
3. See, for example, Chodorow, op. cit., pp. 79–80.
4. See Ross D. Parke, *Fathers* (Cambridge, Massachusetts: Harvard University Press, 1981), especially Chapter I.
5. Alexander Mitscherlich's famous view of the contemporary world as a "society without the father" is, in fact, less than valid. It appears that yesterday's image of the stern Prussian father (upon which Mitscherlich based his observations) has faded. Men today are taking a more central role in childrearing and will in the future have a pronounced (and more benign) effect upon their children if such a trend continues. See Mitscherlich, *Society Without the Father* (New York: Schocken, 1970).
6. Neil Issacs, *Jock Culture* (New York: Random House, 1978), p. 17.
7. Daniel Levinson, *et al.*, *The Seasons of a Man's Life* (New York: Knopf, 1978), p. 36.

CHAPTER 2

"To Play Third Base Again. . . ."

Patriarchy is a dual system, a system in which men oppress women, and in which men oppress themselves and each other. . . . Ultimately, men cannot go any further in relating to women as equals than they have been able to go in relating to other men as equals—an equality which has been so deeply disturbing, has generated so many psychological as well as literal casualties, and which has left so many unresolved issues of competition and frustrated love.

—JOSEPH PLECK, *The American Man*

Just as the juvenile era was marked by a significant change—the development of the need for compeers, for playmates rather like oneself—the beginning of pre-adolescence is equally spectacularly marked . . . by the appearance of a new type of interest in another person. . . . This new interest in the preadolescent era . . . is a specific new type of interest in a particular member of the same sex who becomes a chum or close friend. This change represents the beginning of something very like full-blown psychiatrically defined love.

—HARRY STACK SULLIVAN, *The Interpersonal Theory of Psychiatry*

Besides learning about being men by watching our fathers, we found out about masculinity from our friends. We exchanged secrets, we played at games and sports, and we sometimes shared our awakening sexuality. And yet, as we became adults, we found it increasingly difficult to maintain friendships with other men or to share our lives with them. One of the most central (and most misunderstood) aspects of being a man today, it is a source of much of our uncertainty. As adults we seem to have lost much of our capacity for close friendships, and many of us look with nostalgia to a time when we could be intimate with our male contemporaries and peers.

"My relationships with men are not as close as they were when I grew up," Edward, a successful lawyer, tells me. "It's hard to find people to replace old friends from childhood or the friends you met in college and law school. Everyone seems so busy doing different things today, and it's difficult to relate to men just as men. My wife and I now mostly meet people as couples," Edward continues, "and it usually seems that the women in the relationships are more interesting to both of us, while the men seem more uptight. It generally feels easier to talk with the women in an intimate way."

"Still," Edward wistfully adds, "I miss male friends. In some ways I feel rootless in not having close relationships with other men, and I feel badly that I haven't worked to keep the friendships I had when I was growing up."

Other men express a similar sense of loss and frustration. One said, for example, "Sometimes when I've felt good about a couple of guys and have wanted to get to know them well, I could get just so close and then I'd hit up against a brick wall; at a certain point these men didn't seem to feel comfortable about sharing their thoughts and feelings and about having what I would call an intimate friendship."

In childhood and adolescence, we seek solace and understanding from our male peers, and many of us look for a closeness which we often lacked with our fathers. As psychologist Harry Stack Sullivan noted, an intense early relationship with a "chum," and sometimes with several chums, marks an important transition in our lives, and it constitutes a tentative initial step outside the confines of our immediate family. In sharing equally for the first time with another person, we are able to test our feelings of love in a way that often provides a model for subsequent relationships.[1]

For heterosexual men, male friendship is usually a distinct stage in our ability to love and be intimate with members of the opposite sex. At a certain point in late youth, however, we feel the need to assert a growing heterosexuality and the accompanying denial of homosexual feelings by strictly limiting our intimacy with other young men. In return for the love of women we surrender feelings of closeness with members of our own sex. Today, many men feel uneasy about the outcome. We are realizing that it was not necessary to deny our affection for other men or our need to share with them. Fear of close contact with other men still prevails, however, as does fear of being thought homosexual. We find ourselves Ishmaels clinging to the spars of the sunken Pequod: we can neither chart a way back to our earlier lives, nor can we find a clear route into the future.

As we shall see, men seem to have developed several strategies for dealing with their sense of loss and with the problem of male friendship. The first of these might be called a regressive strategy, as men attempt to recreate the sorts of friendships they had in childhood and youth. We join softball teams or take part in intensely competitive bouts of tennis, or racquetball, or we spend a night out with the "boys." Another more innovative strategy involves taking part in discussion groups with other men to talk of individual experiences and lives. This approach offers opportunities to learn about ourselves as men by reflecting on our assumptions and past behavior. We shall discover, however, that each of these strategies has distinct limitations; there is no easy way to gain intimacy with other men or to better our friendships.

Indeed, male friendship is today generally at a lower ebb than in the past. In the 19th century, for example, the men's fraternal group—either formal or informal—was often an essential feature of social life, and men commonly joined with others at work, in the tavern or cafe during leisure hours, or in the environment of a club.[2] Television beer commercials might today show us convivial portraits of men socializing after a hard shift on the job or out on the town after winning the big case or election to political office. In reality, these popular images of masculine interaction are anachronistic and largely idealized. Most of the trades which T.V. ads so fetchingly portray have been heavily affected by automation. Longshoremen now handle containerized cargo, lumberjacks work with heavy "cherry picker" equipment, steel workers monitor closed electric furnaces, and when middle-class professional men celebrate a raise or promotion, they are more likely to do so with champagne shared at home with the family than—as the ads would have it—with premium beer in a bar full of men. Despite these currently fashionable advertisements and the masculine images they portray, the interaction of adult males is not facilitated by contemporary society in a way it might have been at an earlier time. Indeed, it is ironic that advertising agencies, in creating the images of mass society, portray male relationships as strong and intact at a time when male sociability has been in decline.

If male friendship remains vital and strong, it is not in the friendship we mostly find as adults, but in the male friends we have in youth. The childhood and adolescent group of friends, with its stress on athletic and physical prowess, on banter and carousing, and on strong group identity is a central part of our experience. Many men feel nostalgic about relationships which they had with male friends in their adolescent years. We have lost sight, however, of the fact that Western society at one time ordained such friendships throughout life. If we can understand this, then recovering male friendship, though in suitable form for a changed contemporary world, might not seem so difficult a task. The past provides a model of what is possible, and although most of us would not want to use past lessons as a blueprint, the past keeps alive the possibility of finding alternatives to the present.

My first real experience with male friends came at summer camp. Before then, I had friendships in school, and a best friend, a boy who lived next door and with whom I felt closer than with my own two brothers, who were considerably younger. But until going to camp when I was about ten, I did not have a "gang" of friends. My camp cabin-mates provided a sense of belonging and of closeness. Our lives were centered on the rituals of growing up: on sports—always and especially sports, on play and rivalry, and finally on our awakening sexuality. For boys who were accomplished in sports, athletic competition became a real pleasure, a way to prove ourselves and to gain prestige (as indeed it remains today even among the men who belong to the slow-pitch softball team on which I currently play). Baseball, soccer, touch football, swimming—all could be turned into team competition by our counselors and camp director as we campers learned lessons about the kinds of struggles expected of us as boys in training for manhood. We were instructed in team play, in loyalty to the group, and in winning. Whether or not such "male bonding" in group activity is instinctive, as sometimes claimed,[3] the creation of these athletic bonds served an educational purpose: they introduced us into the world of male camaraderie and male competition.

Our common backgrounds, too, held us together. We all came from New York City and environs during the rock-and-roll revolution of the mid-fifties, and we all shared the new music on A.M. radio; a music introduced by Alan Freed which was ours and which distinguished us from earlier generations; a music which my father had described as sounding "like it came right out of a toilet bowl." And, except for a few eccentrics who rooted for the Philadelphia Phillies, we all followed one of the three New York major league baseball teams (Yankee fans, however, always appeared to be so arrogant! It seemed too easy to root for a team which always won. As I have said, I lived and died for the Dodgers).

Our relationship with camp counselors was another common group experience, since for most of us these counselors were the only men besides our fathers with whom we had ever lived. I can remember being awed by the physical size of these young men—college boys who had landed relatively easy summer jobs—by their hairy chests, by the length of their penises as they urinated at adjacent stalls, by their lewd talk and their references to sexual matters about which we were only dimly aware. My father had never spoken in this way nor had he assumed that I should know such things about female or male anatomy or about what men and women did in bed together. (Actually, I had not yet connected the sex act with bed; I merely knew that a man stuck his thing into a woman's thing, and that this was supposed to feel good and bring a sense of masculine accomplishment. According to our counselors, it was what you did to become a man.)

Counselors also taught us how to swear, as did some of the older boys, but proper knowledge of this masculine art did not happen automatically. Until I was put right by Al, our counselor in cabin ten (a cabin which corresponded to our age), I thought that "balls" referred to female breasts. This seemed logical, of course, but Al corrected me with both ridicule and tenderness, holding me up before my cabinmates as an example of utter stupidity but telling me afterwards how this terminology and the ubiquitous epithet "fuck" should actually be used.

Sex was everywhere in our young lives. The way we learned about sex provides a primary example of the way we were taught to act as men—and eventually to separate ourselves from other men. The great mystery was on our minds constantly, and we attempted to decipher the odds and ends of information and innuendo that we had gathered from older boys or from counselors. The most exciting moments in camp life occurred when we went out together on midnight "raids" to the girls' cabins which were some distance away. Stealth was of the essence, since the authorities banned such raiding parties, but a kind of male hierarchy was created to rank those who had been on the greatest number of forays without being caught. When we arrived at the girls' cabins, there was not much to do, perhaps to see our girlfriends of the moment (these pre-teen alliances were constantly shifting), and then to return home. The excitement was in the illicit quality of the enterprise, an illicitness which was near, I later discovered, to the supposed illicitness of sex itself.

What real sexual contact we had, we had with each other. These were mostly innocent fumblings and sessions of group masturbation at night after lights out. We did not know much about homosexuality, and most of us did not think it wrong to have sexual contact with boys in the next bed to our own. We only knew that it felt good, and that we were discovering a new world of experience. Once, toward the end of the summer when I was eleven or twelve, Al and his assistant counselor rushed into the darkened cabin to discover us during one of these sessions. "You bunch of homos!" he yelled, as he played his flashlight across the scene. Until that moment I had not known that there was anything particularly wrong with what we had been doing, but since the counselors threatened to tell our parents, it dawned on me that we must have transgressed some important social barrier. So began my own homophobia. In interviewing men for this book, I have found many who had similar childhood experiences, who are heterosexual today, and who learned their fear of homosexuality chiefly from the social rejection which discovery entailed.

At this time in our lives, such experimentation was a school for sexuality. One man, Dale, told me the following: "It must have been just before the start of junior high when I would meet secretly with two friends, Ken and Paul, in Ken's garage where we all masturbated together. I can remember a scene a lot like that in Fellini's autobiographical movie, *Amarcord*: the three of us seated in Ken's grandfather's car beating away for dear life. None of us were yet able to reach orgasm, but I can recall that one time Ken yelled out, 'Hey, I got bubbles!' and that I was both impressed and envious at this turn of events. Ken, after all, already had a slight mustache along his upper lip, and he was more developed physically than either Paul or me. To him belonged the honor of entering first into manhood, it seemed."

"Curiously," Dale continues, "none of this seemed especially illicit or shameful to us at the time. We took precautions not to be discovered, of course, but this was mostly because discovery would be embarrassing, not because we were doing something wrong. We were experimenting with our own bodies together, and we were initiating each other as boys into the world of male sexuality. A little while after beginning at junior high, however, we ceased meeting together, and we never again discussed what we had done. I think it was because we suddenly came to realize that we might be thought of as 'queers' by our new and more mature junior-high friends." Instead of making us closer, our greater knowledge of sex and its penalties served to separate us. Our fears of homosexuality and our focus on girls intruded on the male intimacy of our childhood years and led to the distant relations of our adulthood.

In childhood and adolescence, many of us were especially close with a "chum," a single friend with whom we shared our lives, our sexual awakenings, and our inner worlds of feelings. Ed was my first friend, and when I moved with my family to California, I had several others. I realize now that I had a succession of especially close chums—one single male friend at a time—for most of my youth. During high school it was Pete, but our friendship cooled after we became roommates following the memorable ride to college with our fathers. We both understood that we could not live together without constant conflict, and our experiment at rooming together ended after a strife-torn semester in the college dorms. Today I still consider Peter a close friend, but this is little more than a fiction, since we rarely see each other and do not maintain regular contact. Having a chum during adolescence remains important. Even if that friendship has faded, one remains loyal to it in a way that one does not usually remain loyal to a past love relationship with someone of the opposite sex. Men and women may be able to share more closely with each other, but loyalty to the idea of male friendship—and nostalgia for that friendship—runs especially deep among men who have been one-time chums.

Other men have confirmed such feelings, and it might be useful here to look in some detail at a few male friendships.

I. *Stan*

Stan is dark and wiry. His body is muscular and his bushy black beard partially masks a handsome face with chiseled features and striking blue eyes. His eyes betray his Nordic heritage, and they can shift from a penetrating glance to a soft and revealing glow. He talks, as it were, with these eyes, and one cannot help being transfixed by them and drawn deeper into conversation. Stan works as a clinical psychologist and it is clear how his gaze and its frankness serve to assist his therapeutic practice. He is reflective, earnest, and displays an intensity which is deepened by a recent divorce and the pain that he feels from that loss. We have come to know each other through conversations. Stan's experiences follow:

> When I was a kid, I had close relationships with other boys, and I had one friend in particular—Eric. I've known him since we were three years old, and I still have contact with him today. As kids, we were so much alike and did so many of the same things that people thought of us as brothers. That's not a new story of course, but that's what Eric and I were like. We always seemed to be together. But we also had the greatest fights. We'd kill each other in these fights. We'd get into arguments on the football field, sock each other; I gave him a bloody nose once, and he gave me a black eye, but before that day was over we'd be back chumin' it together, walkin' down the street, ridin' our bikes together.
>
> This scene lasted till the middle of high school, and then Eric's family moved one town over from our middle-class suburb into a wealthy neighborhood. His father had become successful in business and started to make the mega-bucks, and he had to have a life-style that reflected his new wealth and status. This turn of events broke up the family though, since Eric's father eventually began running around with women in the city, and his mother filed for a divorce. All of this really scarred Eric, and he seems never to have recovered from the pain of that time. Late in high school he became crazy and got into lots of trouble, doing break-ins, vandalism, smoking pot, turning onto drugs, and finally getting into hard stuff. I remained friends with him and stayed close through this time, and despite all his problems, it still seemed the same when we were together: we still were able to have a good relationship.
>
> We had always been good athletes—the only white boys in the school to make all the teams. Even so, up to this time, Eric was just that much better in everything than I was, always one step ahead. I could never catch up; he was a real natural.
>
> Eric and I had a very close sexual relationship in growing up. We never had homosexual relations, but we discovered our sexuality together and shared it openly. We masturbated for the first time together, and we showed each other how to do it. We had our first sexual contact with a girl together in the woods when we were twelve years old. We shared the fantasies we would have about women, and later we even went to a prostitute together. At fourteen Eric started looking older, and he had a relationship with an eighteen-year-old girl whom he was sleeping with constantly. I wasn't doing that sort of thing. That's when we first started to drift apart. He'd started to spend a lot of time with her and had less time for me.
>
> A couple of years earlier, we were both propositioned by a man at a

Y.M.C.A., and it was only by luck that we didn't get into real trouble. We were both scared shitless and only narrowly escaped from a bad scene. Eric however had a number of homosexual encounters in high school and told me about them. I remember feeling confused, and I thought: "disgusting: that's the worst thing that could ever happen: to have sex with a man." Since that time I have had many other men proposition me, but I've never been attracted to another man and have never had sex with a man, although I've thought a lot about what it would be like. I guess that it's not something that I really want to be involved with.

Today my friend Eric lives in California where he's trying to write screenplays. He'd had a little success at it, but nothing to brag about. He's been through a whole series of things. Coincidentally, my relationship with him still weaves a thin but binding thread through my life. Once, when I was stationed in California in the Army, my sister called to tell me that Eric lived nearby. I hadn't heard from him in almost two years. I called him, we saw each other, and for six or eight months we renewed our close friendship even though we were four hundred miles apart. Then he split up with his wife and drew into himself. The funny thing is that he had married a woman with a child and had a child of his own with her, the very thing I was to do a short time later. In fact, he named his son after me—little Stan. We still have what you might call an intense relationship, although we go for long periods without maintaining contact. I feel at times that Eric is avoiding me, that he's ashamed of himself and of his failures. He's a troubled man, a troubled person. You might look at him as "the bad brother" and me as the "good"; I went the straight and expected route, and he went the narrow and crooked one, I guess.

My experience with Eric has helped me to make contact with new male friends. I learned from Eric that I can still have close relationships with men. Even if my friends don't want to write me, even if they don't want to call me, I can still say "That's okay; that's just where they are in their lives." Once in awhile I would call some of the new men I met when we moved to this part of the country. I didn't feel like I needed this constant input from them, but only some contact, only to know that they thought about me once in awhile. They all seemed to respond to this. People visited me more often. They would invite me to come see them, and we would be able to talk about personal and intimate things and about women and how we were changing. We could begin to develop a dialogue and this has continued. My male friends helped with my divorce and were a kind of support group for me in this difficult time. There was a period when this sort of thing was dormant, but I learned from my relationship with Eric that I could still ask for closeness from men. In that way, my experience with my first close friend was a model for later and present friendships. And I learned also that I had to seek out these friendships. No one was going to do it for me.

Making new contact with men wasn't easy. Sometimes I sensed these men holding back and I felt myself holding back. It's easier for all of us, I guess, to be closer with women. But eventually things did happen because I really pursued it. I wouldn't give it up, and I found a couple of men with whom I became very close and with whom I could talk.

Men seem to begin by finding a topic that has to do with something *outside* themselves. I can talk more easily with women about how I *feel*, but with men I find that I have to talk about how we feel *about* something. One man who comes to mind is my recent friend, David. He's a very gifted musician. Music was our first arena of contact, and it gives us something to talk about. He's a classical guitarist, yet he is very guarded about his talent and will perform only for his family or for me. We were able to build on music (as Eric and I were able to build on sports) to become close friends. Still, I wish it were easier for men to experience intimate friendships rather than depending on some extraneous crutch for contact with each other.

II. *Mike*

When I arrived to interview Mike, he was bathing and diapering his baby daughter. He is what one might call a "new style" liberated man, and he is very conscious and articulate about the process which led him toward rethinking the legacy of his past and establishing a new relationship with his wife and with other men. A teacher, Mike is fond of illustrating his remarks with almost pedagogical detail and of relating anecdotes which might lead the attentive student to grasp the point of today's "lesson." Once he has fed the baby and put her to bed, he is ready to settle down by the woodstove and to talk about his life and the evening's topic: male friendships and their meaning in his life. While Mike's experience parallels Stan's in some ways, it is very different in others. For instance, as a teenager Mike did not build special friendships on the basis of sports and physical prowess but instead sought friends who shared his artistic and creative interests.

I wasn't associated with the athletic crowd in school. I had a close friend who was interested, as I was, in making films way back in the early sixties. He and I shared a lot, especially resentment for the expressed and unexpressed values of the school and the dominance of sports in everyone's lives. My friendship with him was really valuable, and I look back on it (and I think he does too) as a kind of shelter from the oppressive values that were being rammed down our throats there. I think we had a pretty intimate friendship. I remember shared feelings and that we became vulnerable to each other. There were no false fronts.

I've never had a lot of friends, but the few I had were close. These have always been the friends with whom I've spent time and shared experiences. In college I also had one very close male friend, but what's strange is that I haven't heard from him in years. What is especially weird is that *I* think we were closer than he thinks we were. I valued that college friendship and have tried to maintain it, but he doesn't respond to my letters. The friend I had in high school reinforced the opposition I felt to existing values; the one in college served much less in this way, and I think that when I became more independent and even somewhat radical in the late sixties, it drove my college friend and me apart.

This was a real disappointment, because I thought I would be close to this college friend for the rest of my life, and our paths have since diverged. I was inspired by him—he was a very creative guy. We were roommates for a year, and felt good about our friendship. But after college we both changed, and he made it clear that he didn't want the kind of closeness that I wanted. He returned to a more traditional view of what manhood is, and I just didn't see him much anymore.

It is sad for me to realize that we can probably never be close again. We don't share now as we did then, and that's been a real loss. And there are some other examples of guys I wanted to get to know well, but they seemed to have felt afraid of being close with another man or just didn't have enough time to work at developing intimate, supportive friendships. Now I am at the point of seeking a more formal arrangement which would allow me to share my thoughts and feelings with other men, and I have finally decided to be part of an ongoing men's support group.

I guess that other more traditional men might think I am strange. In fact, my next door neighbor, who works for the gas company, just can't believe what I do in my marriage and around the house. He and I have become friendly in the last year or so, and it's fun to see the expression on his face when he finds out some of the things I've been doing to change my life. He came over one day, for example, when I was hanging up diapers on the line and said half jokingly, "You better not let your neighbors see you doing that." This guy, you understand, is in his late forties and has three kids and a very traditional marriage. He just doesn't know what to make of me. He doesn't come out with hostility at all, but just very frankly tells me that I am really strange. He also conveys a sense of pity for me in that he thinks I am not able to make it in a man's world. When he asks me why I do the laundry, or take care of the baby, or make dinners, I tell him that times have changed. The way he did it was fine for him but I see things a little differently. He's a guy who works hard and feels good about that. He's a provider and wants just to come home, put his feet up, drink a beer, watch T.V., and be waited on. That's the way he's always done things, and that's what he thinks is right and good in America. He also feels okay about coming over and talking with me. We share the traditional male topics: sports, or when I work on my car, which is frequent, he comes over with suggestions and sometimes helps me do the work. We have a friendship, a conventional one you might say, but it's a friendship, nevertheless. Still, he has an interest sometimes in why I've chosen to do what I do, at other times there's almost a trace of ridicule and even defensiveness in what he says. I think that I create what might be called "cognitive dissonance" for him: he sees me working on my car or putting a new roof on the house, and he also sees me taking care of a baby and doing housework. He doesn't know what to make of it or how to continue a friendship with me. All that information feeds in and just goes 'tilt' for him. Basically, I think he likes me, but I leave him really perplexed.

It's interesting that I have another friend next door on the other side of the house, who's now a member of my men's group. He's involved at the university health-care services and he does workshops on male sexuality. So he's very much interested in the changes I am describing. When I explain to him some of the things I am doing, and when we share our thoughts and feelings in the group, he tells me, "You're really a person of the future!" Isn't that strange? I have one neighbor telling me that I am cuckoo, and another saying that I represent something that may be the wave of the future—something more people should emulate.

Some methods which men are utilizing to strengthen ties have been innovative and others have been traditional. Male support groups of the kind to which Mike belongs represent the "innovative" path. In contrast, traditional sports and athletics continue to provide a conventional outlet for our needs to band together and might be seen as a kind of "regressive" strategy to promote friendship. Today, men are participating in sports as never before. They are playing racquetball, squash, tennis, and softball in unprecedented numbers, while competition in marathons and road races continues to increase, as does interest in weightlifting and body-building. In one sense, this sports explosion is attributable to a new awareness of health and to the rewards which our society provides for those who remain perpetually young. But the sports explosion also owes much, I believe, to a male desire to be with other men and to insulate themselves through the old verities of male life.

Something of this sort was implied by one of the members of my own softball team who expressed surprise that over twenty-five men had signed up for this year's team—nearly a third more than last season. In a mock-serious tone, he said that he guessed the cause of this large turnout was "those beer commercials on the tube: those ads make it look good for men to be together. And after the game we can all go out and drink beer as a team, almost as if *we* were on T.V." This got a laugh from the others who were listening, but I thought I detected a sense among us that the idea wasn't such a bad one after all.

Yet, it is clear that finding a refuge in athletic competition and in team sports provides no real solution. Banding together in this way is inherently regressive: it carries us back to a mythological and secure past but it does not ask us to grow. In returning to little boys' games, we become, in some ways, little boys. There is safety in playing third base on the softball team, and I find myself shouting encouragement to the pitcher, congratulating a scoring runner, or yelling at the umpire in the same way I did at age nine on my first Little League team. There are other dangers, as well: it reinforces our need for traditional achievement and our conventional fears of failure which sports promote. This traditional setting sometimes almost guarantees the return of pressures to perform in a "masculine" way to win the esteem of male peers.

I would like to quote directly from a journal entry which I made on the night that we played our opening game of the season:

> When I didn't start tonight I found myself feeling slighted, and devalued, and reacting in much the same why as I did whenever I didn't get to start as a kid or during a high school game. After a while, however, I was able to overcome some of these feelings and to sit on the bench with Paul, Billy, Ed, and Larry. All of them are good ball-players and each was faced with resisting what must have seemed a blow to his own self-image. There we sat and rooted for our side, joking on the bench and watching as our warriors played their innings in the field and then took their turns at bat. By the bottom of the fourth, the score was tied at five runs apiece, and then I went in at third base, feeling elated and nervous when Stefan, our manager, called on me. (Stefan, by the way, had brought his two-year-old son with him and was not only playing second base and managing, but was doing child care between innings

as well: a decidedly modern role for a man in this traditional world of male combat.)

As soon as I got on the field, I felt my mouth go dry and I experienced a sense of dread: "How will I handle the first grounder?" I thought. "What a phony I am. I haven't played third base in years. What if I screw up? I'll just have to ask to be taken out. I've got much better things to occupy me than to be standing out here under the lights. I could be home accomplishing something valuable. I could be working on the house or writing my book." By the time the pitcher went into his wind-up, I was completely psyched and anxiety ridden, feeling driven at all costs to make good as a "man" and so to retain the esteem of my friends.

The infield was all chewed up. The stadium lights barely illuminated the playing surface, and I thought of using all of this as an excuse to cover a bad performance, and I also fought to overcome the impulse to make excuses. In sports, I thought, excuses don't count: either you can make the play or you can't. In fact, that's the beauty of it and partly why we play. We're here to perform, to be part of a male team, and to gain a sense of the sheer pleasure of physical action, and maybe also we're here to show off for the crowd (which by this time was surprisingly large).

There were runners on first and third when I got my chance to handle the ball. I went to my right on a hard grounder, and to my surprise I came up with the ball *barehanded*, but by the time I fielded it, I had no play at home, and no play to second or first. I felt like a real idiot and hung my head, but I was elated that at least I made the stop. On my next opportunity, I couldn't find the handle on another hard shot to third, and I blew a perfect double-play situation, never even getting the ball out of my glove. I felt like a total failure.

By the last inning of the game, we were down six runs (eleven-to-five), and I got a chance to "rehabilitate" myself. It was my first time at bat and I hit a solid single into the outfield. It felt great to make contact and to hear my teammates cheering. At least I could do something well: at least I could show them that I deserved to be on this team. That inning, in fact, we rallied for five runs and might have had more if not for a bad running play which ended our comeback. Even though we fell short, it felt good just to be a part of this rally.

After the game, my teammates complimented me on my hit, and since we had lost by only one run, our confidence was restored and we all went off the field with jokes and congratulations. I am still not sure why I felt so bad doing poorly in the infield, but clearly my concern for my image as a man and an achiever, and for being well-liked by other

> men played a part. When I got home, Sara couldn't believe that I took it all so seriously, but she said that she now understood why my son, Jake, feels so nervous before he competes for his playground team, and where he must have learned his nervousness and his need for athletic accomplishment: messages about maleness and male achievement are transmitted from father to son, from generation to generation, in ways which we have not yet begun to comprehend.

Today, many men wish friendly relationships with each other and are more willing than they were, even a short time ago, to seek them out. Some go about this in a traditional manner (by engaging in competitive sports, for example), and gain the conventional emotional release. The goal-oriented and competitive structure of sports allows us to regulate our distance from others. We can draw back and concentrate on the task at hand, behaving merely as a team member. The penalty for this, of course, is that individual feelings and needs remain largely unexpressed and are restricted by traditional roles.

A less orthodox and thus more threatening, but potentially more rewarding, way to share with other men has been opened by the movement to create male support and "consciousness-raising" groups. These provide a deliberate alternative to more traditional ways of establishing friendships between men. We might recall that Mike, the man with whom we spoke earlier, belongs to one of these groups. In discussing his group experience, he provides us with insights into reasons why men engage in such activities, what they can gain from men's groups, and what problems such groups confront.

> When we began the group we had about a dozen guys as members. We started through a newspaper article about local male support groups and an organization that sets them up. We all responded to the ad to be part of a group, and initially we were provided with a facilitator—a professional who could lead us. Soon, however, we didn't need to rely on an outside facilitator anymore. Things went okay for awhile, but within six months about half the men had dropped out of the group. Some had completely different expectations about what they thought the group should be. A couple of men were having serious problems that were beyond the scope of the group to confront. There was also one guy who thought we should always be talking about how we oppress women. Other people didn't feel that way, however. They thought that this was part of it, but they felt that much of what they wanted in the

group was a place to begin to explore intimacy, to share feelings, and to help each other through various ups and downs, and to grow in a number of different ways.

Our membership has been constant at about a half-dozen for over a year now. Each week when we meet, everyone first checks in and talks about what's been happening in their lives. People have always had ongoing issues. Sometimes they're very big and important kinds of issues: my mother's death was one. Another guy was in the process of getting married and was going through changes as a result; another guy went through a long and very difficult custody battle. So there have been big events, but perhaps more typically, we talk about our daily lives and our relationships with other men and women, our work, our frustrations, our fantasies, and so on. After everyone has had a chance to check in, there's a general discussion of some of these issues, and then, before we break up, there's a time for checking out, a time to talk about the process of the evening; what feelings people had when certain things were going on, or we'll talk about the tone of the meeting and what we learned from what people discussed. I think that the men in this group are more intimate with each other than ninety-five percent of the relationships I normally have with men, and we take a lot of risks in revealing ourselves to each other. But there are limits. Some of these limits we have defined and discussed; others we haven't. There are some things that we avoid talking about, and some which are hazy and still evolving.
I haven't felt, however, that those limits are serious enough to prevent me from getting a lot out of the group. I think that the limits are there because it takes a long time for people to learn to trust each other, and to open up as a result of that trusting relationship. I consider the men in the group to be very close friends, but curiously we don't socialize much outside of the group. It's sort of been nice to just keep it a separate and special part of life, not to be confused with any other parts of the daily routine.

Men's groups often prove to be rather time-limited arrangements. "We weren't the most natural group of people to choose to be ongoing friends," Marty tells me, about his experience in a group which has broken up. "We shared politics and work, and when we had exhausted the possibilities of discussing these, there was very little that bound us together. We were not natural friends. We liked each other, but we did not have close relationships outside of the group, and we hadn't been through close experiences together."

"This group died a slow death," he went on. "We had been sustained over a long time by a member who needed support through a divorce, and the last part of the group was involved in dealing with his problems on a weekly basis. At the end, there was some bad feeling between him and one of the group members he felt had been rather callous about his dilemma. The group declined after that, though it seemed finally to end when a number of us left for research trips and to take jobs elsewhere. At the beginning, we had gone through a number of big issues, for example, how we felt about sexuality and how we felt about the women's movement. Then we all gave an extended history of our own lives. When we started to deal with things that were happening in the present, tensions between us were exposed which helped put an end to the group. We flirted with putting it on a firmer footing by discussing some of this process, but we were never able to."

My own experience in men's groups, I should note, has been rather similar to Marty's. Two groups to which I have belonged began over issues raised by the women's movement and its critique of male behavior. Most of us were involved with women who were defining their own roles and who, in essence, asked for a redefinition of our relationships. We men felt the need to explore these questions and to give and receive support, criticism, and understanding. We also needed to appreciate each other as men and to begin to break down the distance between us. As with Marty's group, we spoke first about "big issues": about our relationships with men and women, about the sexist assumptions with which we had grown up. We talked about work and politics, we tried to share some of our feelings with each other, and we each took time to talk about our own life histories. When we had exhausted these possibilities, we were forced to deal with the present and with our feelings about the group itself. We were also faced with giving meaningful support to other group members. We discussed divorce—a perennial subject in men's groups—and the daily dilemmas of careers and relationships. It was then that the groups began to dissolve. As in Marty's case, the groups to which I belonged seemed to drift apart, as we all found other and more "compelling" things to do with our time. I am convinced, in looking back, that many of us—myself included—invented whatever reasons we could for leaving the group. Sustaining intimate contact and dealing on a close and personal basis proved to be too difficult for us. We seemed, in effect, to reach a barrier of self-revelation which we were not equipped to transcend. We all wanted to share our feelings and thoughts with other men, but when that opportunity arrived, we withdrew in self-defense. That defensiveness prevented many of us from remaining friends after our group experience ended.

All this shows, I think, the sheer difficulty of maintaining formal men's-group relationships and of learning what these groups have to teach. It also shows how our ambivalence about being close to other males carries over from adolescence to adulthood. A few years ago, Warren Farrell and Marc Festeau wrote of the coming of a putative "men's liberation" and assured us that all would be well if we would just join together, share our experience and feelings, help each other overcome our inherent sexism, and provide some mutual support.[4] In reality, however, this has not been easy to accomplish. Some men's groups have been able to continue. Many have not. Our resistance to being intimate with each other is more deeply ingrained than we imagined. Yet many of us have learned from our group experience, and many of us say that we would join such groups again. We have a need to be with other men, to have male friends, and to share our experience. In a sense, we all want to play third base again; yet, we also want to grow. We still resist intimate friendships with other men, and this is part of the ambivalence about our masculinity. We look fondly at our childhood as a time of closer connection with members of our own sex, but we find it difficult to recover that sense of closeness. Indeed, this is only one portion of the divided feelings which we have in many other areas of our lives; whether in our relationships with women, in our perceptions about work, or in our experience as parents.

Notes

1. Harry Stack Sullivan, *The Interpersonal Theory of Psychiatry* (New York: Norton, 1953), especially Chapters 16–17.
2. On the historical role of the male peer group, see especially Edward Shorter, *The Making of the Modern Family* (New York: Basic Books, 1975), pp. 206ff, and Elizabeth H. Pleck and Joseph H. Pleck, *The American Man* (Englewood Cliffs, New Jersey: Prentice-Hall, 1980), especially Chapters 8–9.
3. See, for example, Lionel Tiger, *Men in Groups* (New York: Random House, 1969).
4. Warren Farrell, *The Liberated Man* (New York: Bantam, 1975); Marc Feigen Fasteau, *The Male Machine* (New York: McGraw-Hill, 1974).

CHAPTER 3

Men and Women: The Early Years

. . . For virtually every human, the central infant-parent relationship, in which we form our earliest, intense and wordless feelings toward existence, is a relationship with a woman . . .

—Dorothy Dinnerstein,
The Mermaid and the Minotaur

So go ahead, love her! Be brave! Here is fantasy begging you to make it real! So erotic! So wanton! So gorgeous! Glittery perhaps, but a beauty nonetheless! Where we walk together, people stare, men covet, and women whisper. . . . Vanity? Why not! Leave off with the blushing, bury the shame, you are no longer your mother's naughty little boy! Where appetite is concerned, a man in his thirties is responsible to no one but himself.

—Philip Roth, *Portnoy's Complaint*

Sara and I were in a restaurant having a late dinner after a long day at our jobs. We were both concerned about the demands that our work made on our time together, about the difficulty of balancing our own careers against the need to be with each other and to build our relationship. Suddenly, I retaliated in frustration to her request that I devote more time to our common tasks and to our love together. "Despite everything," I blurted out, "I still really want a woman who will give in to my demands and who will mainly take care of me—a woman who I can pretty much control." The combination of fatigue and a good bottle of wine had unleashed my secret. Sara smiled with silent triumph and also with a kind of gentle understanding, for I had confirmed something that she had long suspected. In the face of my advocacy of a shared and equal relationship and despite my acceptance of many lessons of the women's movement, I had violated my self-professed beliefs and had shown myself to be something of a sexist and a hypocrite.

And yet, in looking back on that incident, I suspect that I had acted less as a hypocrite than as a man wrestling with dilemmas that today confront many of us. Even though we might want our relationships with women to be based on concepts of equality and a sharing of work and income, of child rearing and house care, as well as on honesty about our feelings and emotions, we still balk at actual sharing and equality when the going gets a bit rough. We all have a backlog of male experience which leads us to expect that our relationships with women will mainly be unequal. Although many of us have experienced great changes in recent years, it has been difficult for us to break completely with old roles and expectations. In our relationships with the women that we love, we still often expect to be accorded a privileged and dominant position.

How did these ambivalent feelings develop? Why do so many of us want to behave differently with women and yet cannot do so? In comparing my experience with that of other men, it became clear that our expectations about women arose from several sources. We acquired our fathers' views about what it is to be a man, as well as what it is to be a man dealing with women; we learned further lessons from male friends. In addition, we learned from our relationships with our own mothers, and from the way we saw our mothers interact with our fathers. Finally, we learned from encounters with girlfriends during our adolescent years. We have already talked about our fathers and male friends. Now let us look at the other sources.

Our relationship with our mothers, psychologists tell us, is laden with divided feelings. From the time we are infants we desire closeness with our mothers, but at some point we begin to resist them and to declare ourselves masculine and strong rather than feminine and weak. The process by which boys become men in our society demands that we overtly suppress our feminine and "softer" sides, even though we may secretly long to return to the dependence and passivity we first experienced with our mothers. Mothers help encourage this sense of ambivalence and division. On one hand, they enjoy us as cuddly, dependent children and as young males whose love is unconditional. On the other hand, our mothers want us to become independent and masculine, able to make our way in the world and to act like "real" men. We, and our mothers too, are pulled and tugged by the double nature of our relationship, and this divided set of expectations haunts not only our childhood, but our adult years as well. Just as we can no longer rely on lessons our fathers taught us to negotiate a changing world, so we can no longer draw sustenance from the expectations of our mothers.[1]

I noted earlier that some of my experiences with my own mother were shaped by the circumstances which confronted men and women shortly after World War II. From the time I was about a year old, my father—as I've said—was away in the U.S. Navy, and with no effort of my own I thus fulfilled the primal fantasy of exiling a father to dominate the love of a mother. And since my mother and I lived in an apartment directly above that of my grandparents, my life began with a virtual monopoly of the sometimes smothering love of mother and grandmother: a garden of Eden not easily recovered, but one I longed to regain in later years.

At my birth my mother had more than the usual share of the pangs and throes of parturition, and this, I believe, helped to heighten some of the ambivalent feelings in our relationship. During her pregnancy she had chosen an obstetrician who believed in the methods of Grantly Dick-Read, one of the earliest advocates of "natural" childbirth. Those were the days, however, before the French gynecologist, Fernand Lamaze, attempted to lessen pain through pre-labor training and exercise.

The followers of Dick-Read thought that childbirth could be a "beautiful" experience for mother and child if mental concentration were practiced. There was little concern for educating expectant mothers, and as a result my mother gave birth to me without either preparation or the use of medication; the experience was anything but "beautiful" and she described it as perhaps the most painful moment of her life. My mother anticipated the birth of her first child believing that as a woman she must sacrifice for her children's welfare; the pain of childbirth was part of the sacrifice. As I grew up the message was reinforced, and I came to feel it was her place to cater to my whims and needs. She must have resented my demands and the social injunction that mothers must do for their children, but, as befitted the image of the "good" mother in our society, she expressed very little of her feelings about this.

As a child I learned about relationships with women by watching my mother and father. She took care of him, preparing his dinner every night, although she did not like to cook and had a deep and abiding fear of any kitchen operation more complex than boiling eggs. He would barely clear his throat and she would be ready with another helping of flank steak or a second cup of coffee, anticipating his needs before he seemed to realize them himself. The house was always clean, the dishes washed, the shopping done, and my mother seemed to perform these essential but tedious chores as if they required little effort and less time. An intelligent and capable woman, she took no interest in developing a career of her own, but, like most women of her generation, she remained at home to provide for the physical and emotional needs of her husband and family. Work, for her, would have connoted a loss of standing in the world: women who did not *need* to work seemed the freest for her and her generation. Going out to work represented an admission that a woman's husband could not support his family, and that he was, in fact, less than a man.

When I return today to my parents' house for a visit, my mother takes care of me in much the same ways that she did when I was young. She washes my laundry without my asking, she goes out of her way to prepare my favorite foods and to stock the refrigerator with things she knows I'll like, and what is more important, she seems to anticipate my emotional needs. The point, however, is not necessarily that my mother has been subservient to her husband and her sons, but that her relationship with her husband and with her children functioned well on traditional lines. She cooked, cleaned, and provided emotional support while he earned the income and took care of major items of home maintenance. Such a relationship proved adequate in an earlier time, and I suppose that it still succeeds for some people today. Yet among a growing number of couples these old rules of interaction no longer seem to fit. We want to be able to share more in the everyday chores of survival, in the earning of income, and in our affective lives, as well.

Psychologists and other researchers tell us that the mother-son relationship differs from that of mothers and daughters. Social scientist Nancy Chodorow indicates that mothers in our society tend to treat boys from birth not as genderless infants but as young males, while they treat daughters as beings who are less detached and separate from themselves.[2] As a result, sons develop a more fixed set of boundaries between themselves and the world, and they also come to expect that they will form unique relationships in which women accord them special care. Such expectations carry over into later life, as Columbia University sociologist, Mirra Komarovsky, shows in her excellent study,

Dilemmas of Masculinity. She points out that young males often desire relationships with women who are strong, "liberated," and independent, and yet they also want these same women to treat them with deference and care and to support their masculine needs and wishes.[3] Such young men have come to accept the recent goal of "liberation" from sexual stereotyping; but they have been unable to transcend expectations created by their parents' behavior and by the early bond between mother and son. Many of us who claim to want relationships with independent and self-sustaining women still must contend with the examples that our mothers provided and with our abiding feelings that women should take care of our basic needs.

A number of men whom I interviewed have spoken to me of this dilemma and of the difficulty of moving beyond the expectations we absorbed about womanliness from our mothers. Daniel, a young lawyer, described his experience:

> My mother always deferred to my father and this helped give me the belief that the man is the ruler of the home. I learned as a child that men are the initiators and that women wait to be asked. Over the past few years, however, I have begun to change these expectations: I can now begin to let women initiate, I can let them ask me to dance, to go out on a date. And I have also come to feel even more strongly that it's important for women to have work and careers. I remember feeling when I was young that it was sad that my mother had so much time on her hands at home and didn't continue her career after marriage and that she would have been happier with a job outside the house.
>
> Still I must confess I keep a double standard about women. Maybe it's because my relationship with my mother still has a strong emotional hold on me and maybe I've never separated from her. I see women at the office maintaining their careers, and I think this is all to the good, but in the back of my mind I still think that a woman should take care of a man. I continue to have this image of a perfect woman who will be all things. I would like a woman who is beautiful, who is competent, who has a career, who is sensitive and is a good lover, and who can give me plenty of attention. At the same time she will also be able to cook, to keep the house, to take good care of our kids, and she won't make many demands on me other than slowly to open me up to other sides of myself.
>
> This image, of course, is a real joke, but I'm stuck with it. This woman is an idealized being who will complete me in some ways: she'll be a woman like my mother, and this is an immature hope; she'll also be

someone I can complement and who can complement me. Maybe this is a more mature ideal for a relationship. At the same time, not finding this woman means that I have some serious trouble in letting myself be intimate with the women whom I know and care for. In fact, I think that I often use this idealized image to prevent myself from becoming too close with real women and to avoid my fear of being swallowed up in a relationship in the way I felt swallowed up by my mother.

Sam Doucet, the psychotherapist, has had similar experience:

Sometimes I catch myself adopting attitudes that still hang on but don't come out much in my daily life: the idea, for example, that I should really be more important than my wife. In fact, this is something that my mother did for my father—she made him seem big and strong and the one who did all the thinking in the family. Part of my shock when she died a few years ago was that I then began seeing my father just as he was and not as what she built him up to be. However, I still keep these early images rumbling around in a sort of crazy way, and although I try to put the previous models of my mother and father aside, they're still present in my mind. Today when my wife, Paula, and I have a fight, these old messages usually are responsible for about three-quarters of my anger: the feeling, for example, that I'm being deprived by a woman who is going to take something away from me, which was an old issue between my father and mother.

Once, when I was between jobs, and Paula was supporting us, I began to feel not like a man, but like a little boy who still needed his mother to take care of him, and, in fact, this confusion of past and present has been the source of some real friction between Paula and me. It's an old model that seems to get played out in the present, and which now sometimes leads to resentment between my wife and me.

Another man tells me about how his expectations of his mother affected his subsequent relationships with women. "Until I really thought deeply about it," he says, "I couldn't actually share myself much with women. I felt that I needed to maintain distance and that I couldn't risk a close relationship with a woman without in some way making her into my mother and becoming dependent upon her."

"During that time," he continues, "I actually lived with a woman for two years, but I couldn't let myself get too close, and consequently, the relationship failed. Then, I just went out and had casual sexual affairs with women, and I also had women friends with whom I had no sexual involvement. I separated these relationships, because I thought that getting too involved threatened making the woman I was with into the image of my mother. This would put me at a definite disadvantage—not at all like a man who could share equally with a woman."

Many of us, in fact, experience similar feelings. We still want to be taken care of and emotionally supported by women, yet we struggle against becoming too reliant upon them. This is a legacy of our relationships with our mothers and of our inability to renounce earlier expectations in order to become neither dependent upon the women in our lives nor dominant with them. It is clearly one of the most complex issues haunting contemporary men, and it is one which many of us have yet to resolve.

If we formed expectations of women through our mothers, other attitudes were shaped by our first encounters with the girls of our adolescence and youth. As we grew up, it was clear that as boys we learned different lessons about sexuality and love than those learned by our girlfriends. For boys, sex often seemed an end in itself and a means to succeed in a competitive masculine world. By convincing a girl to have sex—to "make" them, to get them to "put out"—we gained status among our male friends, and we could begin to think of ourselves as accomplished males. We either "scored" or we "failed." Our guideline for behavior never was to become emotionally committed. We tried to get as much as we could while giving as little of ourselves as possible. The goal was to be a "cocks-man" who could screw myriads of girls (or could say that he did) without ever having to love any of them—to be a member, as we said, of the "Four F" club: find 'em, feel 'em, fuck 'em, and forget 'em.

For girls, however, sexuality was expressed less directly and was often used as an emblem of one's feminine attractiveness and as a device to capture and hold a male. Girls seemed to act less interested in the pleasures of sex and certainly less in the notoriety sex afforded than they were in their social popularity and in their standing as desirable female objects. According to the rules of the game, girls who valued themselves needed to avoid sexual encounters as much as possible and to concentrate their main efforts on having and keeping boyfriends. From this, in turn, stemmed our own underlying disrespect for those girls whom we actually persuaded to "put out." If they could have held us by any other means they would have done so, and to sleep with us was actually an admission—we thought—of their inferiority. We discovered, as well, that despite our preconceptions, the girls with whom we actually had sex seemed as interested in it as ourselves; they often seduced us as readily as we attempted to seduce them. The double standard served as the basis for many of our expectations about the women in our lives and for their expectations about us. It is not very surprising that our adult relationships—founded, as they are, upon our earlier beliefs—are often filled with ambiguity and doubt.

For me, the image of male proficiency served as a guide when it came time to experience my initial full-fledged sexual encounter. During most of my early teenage years, I had played around with female classmates at parties or at their homes when their parents were out without having gone "all the way." Now, just barely sixteen and with my newly-minted driver's license, I was determined to say that I had gone to bed with a girl. The one I hoped to corral for this escapade was Eileen, a short and well-built blonde who had rubbed against me behind the laboratory tables in my tenth grade science class, and who I had then visited a few times when her parents had been away. I had heard talk from my friends about what an "easy lay" she was supposed to be, and I called her for a date with the thoughts that I would drive up to a lovers' lane in the hills above the city, where I would move to the real thing. On the big night, my plan (possibly for the first and only time) went just as I had imagined. Parked in a secluded spot, Eileen and I got into the back seat of my Ford where she proceeded virtually to undress me and to show me what it was all about. I remember that just before we finally reached the crucial moment, she asked me if I had brought a rubber. Shivering in the cold night air, I rummaged for the old Trojan which had long impressed its ring on the leather of my wallet in preparation for just such a moment. Then, after some amateurish fumbling on my part, she guided me into her body, and I came almost immediately, flooded by the feeling that, My God! this was really it and yes, it felt as good as it was supposed to, but why did it last so short a time? And, Man! won't I have a lot to tell my friends?

In fact that was just what I did. In school I let it be known to a few trusted comrades what had happened the night before, and after the word of my indiscretion got back to her, Eileen never spoke to me again. She was more than glad to help initiate me into the joys and mysteries of sex, but one paid the penalty of blabbing too much. Her reputation—never very good—was now even further compromised, and she'd be damned if she would be dragged down even more by my bragging about what I had done. For me that was almost the main point: to have sex with her, and then to achieve notoriety by telling my friends. Years later I realized that Eileen had given me a real gift by conducting my initiation, and that I in turn had added only one more blow to the many that she probably bore for being less than a "nice" girl. That was the code, however, by which one grew up. We never thought about the meaning of the rules or about why they should be enforced.

Men learned the lessons of sexuality in a variety of ways during their adolescent years. Some had experiences similar to my own, and others were initiated in different ways. For many of us, however, these encounters reinforced our feelings of male superiority and our belief that women would do our bidding.

Stan and I are sitting in front of the wood stove in his pleasant apartment. We have been talking of our boyhoods and adolescence and of our first awakening to sex. Stan's first experience was frightening.

> The first time I really made love I was about fifteen, and it was real scary. I was sure that I had her pregnant because I had a rubber but I didn't use it. It was in my wallet for about umpteen years and I couldn't believe that this girl—Susan was her name—would go through with what she promised to do with me. She just kept saying yes every step of the way, and I just kept going, trying to fake like I knew what I was doing. So I felt her up, I took her bra off, and I thought, "Wow! Incredible!" and she never said no. Then we got undressed, and neither of us knew what we were doing. I thought of using the rubber, but I was concerned that if I stopped any place she would say no, and I'd lose my big chance. So I just went ahead and did it, and I came right away. I was really worried that she was pregnant, but she had her period right on time, and all my fears about how to tell my parents and what to do were suddenly lifted. After that we made love a lot, and she would ask me not to say anything to anyone. I told her I wouldn't. But, of course, I told my best friend, Eric, about it, and I still swore to her that I hadn't told a soul. Being dishonest in this way was what you were supposed to do in those days.
>
> Following this first experience, Susan and I would fuck all the time and

this was all there was to our relationship. We'd fuck in her car, we'd fuck in my car, we'd fuck in the daytime, in the night, at her house, or at mine. She even wanted to do it in school one day underneath the stairs. I told her I couldn't because I was too afraid of getting caught.

I don't know what was wrong with me; I'd never used birth control at all with her even after that first scare. I just pulled it out before I came, and somehow this always seemed to work. The pill had just been invented, but we couldn't get it, and I was too lazy to use a rubber, or else we both denied what was going on. She had a few late months where we'd both again be climbing the walls, but somehow we never seemed to learn. Her father, I should say, was pretty much a crazy man, and I don't know what he would have done—let alone my own parents—if she'd become pregnant. One time Susan and I were making love upstairs and her parents came home unexpectedly (I guess that everyone has had at least one experience of this kind). Somehow, I pulled up my pants and got out onto the roof, just like in the movies. Her father ran upstairs to see what she was doing, and then he ran outside and searched all around. Luckily, he never looked up to where I was hiding, and when he went back into the house, I jumped off the roof and got away. I couldn't believe what had happened, and I made it to the local bowling alley where I met my friends. Even though I felt loyal to her, I let one or two of my cronies know what had gone on. It was too good a story to keep to myself, and I knew that it would enhance my standing among the boys.

Not all of us, however, were as concerned with attaining manhood through our sexual reputations, and not everyone followed what might seem almost stereotypical patterns of male conquest and bravado. Ted Morgan, the building contractor, tells me, for example, that

I didn't actually go to bed with a girl until I was a sophomore in college, and I don't remember that it was something that I had to do to establish my adulthood or anything like that. I didn't feel like the "odd-person-out" since many of my friends were the same way. My mid-Western background promoted a fairly standard traditional sexual ethic, and although part of me was very enticed by the prospect of fucking, I didn't feel a lot of pressure about it.

I had a regular sequence of girlfriends in high school and the first year of college, and the most we ever did was general touching and feeling. The first time that I ever actually had intercourse was with an exchange student from a woman's college that I met at a party. I attended an all-male school, and I remember thinking, "Man!, it's really great having all these women here." I really didn't have to do anything, in fact. She picked me up, took me back to her room, and put me to bed, and I remember being surprised that the whole thing was so easy. We laid around and made out; at some point we took off our clothes and I got on top of her. Then she just slipped me right into her and instantly I came, Boom! just like that. I was so surprised that I just didn't think about birth control or anything. I was a virgin, after all, and not really up with those things.

In high school and later in college, I don't remember having any sense about who was a virgin and who wasn't. We never talked too much about who was doing what to whom, and although in high school there were a couple of women who actually got pregnant, they always had been with "older guys"—college guys—and not with us. I hear people talking about male settings where men sit around and brag about their sexual conquests, but I've just never been in a circle like that. I can remember times in college when someone would have a date for the weekend and after the woman left, the man would walk around with a smile on his face and make cryptic remarks, but I can never remember being with a group of men in a locker room or dormitory where the basic content of the discussion was crude sexual quantification. I always wondered whether I just missed this sort of discussion or was this really a much less common event than the usual mythodology implies.

Many of us seem to have made the conventional distinction between the "good" girls with whom we went steady, and the girls to whom we went primarily for sex. This distinction was a persistent remnant of the Victorian dual standard of male and female behavior which had prevailed with more or less strength for at least a century. We sought to dominate both "good" girls and "bad" ones, a dominance which we assumed would prepare the way for continued adult control. Those who actually became sexual partners we could threaten with exposure and loss of reputation. Those who were "good" girls became accomplices in a subtle kind of exchange. They were potential marriage partners, and as such could present themselves as "pure," untainted, and worthy of male protection and support. We, at the same time, could expect eventually to become the sole possessors of our wives' sexuality, and, in addition, we could equate these "good" girls in some respects with our mothers: we could seek to monopolize their love and expect them to provide for our emotional needs.

In practice, however, the distinction between "good" and "bad" girls often threatened to break down. Until my first years of college if I did not actually go to bed with my steady girlfriends, I experienced almost everything with them but actual intercourse. It was only through the most blatant sophistry that these steady girlfriends—the "good" girls of high school—could count themselves untainted and that my careful male categorization of womankind could be maintained.

Such was the experience of male contemporaries, as well. Dale, for example, told me that, "I can remember that once when I was about 14 I showed my erect penis to my junior high school sweetheart. We were both pretty innocent, just learning about each other's bodies and there was a real sweetness to our experimental play together. Right before I left for camp for the summer, she asked if she could look at my thing, because she had never seen what a hard one was like, and I complied. I remember how frightened and surprised she seemed as she almost physically shrank back from me. I guess she was afraid that she might someday actually have intercourse with one of those, as enlarged and swollen as it must have seemed to her. But she also had a fascination with it, I think, and with the first awakenings of sex."

Stan, with whom we spoke earlier, tells me that after he had the long-standing sexual relationship with Susan, he became interested in being more serious, in "having a relationship with a girl who was pleasant and who I wanted to be with and who wanted to be with me all the time." Stan notes that

> It wasn't that I was necessarily thinking of finding someone whom I eventually might marry, but only of whether the relationship might continue. I remember that it was then that I went steady with a girl—Amanda—who I had known since elementary school. I gave her a ring to wear around her neck, but I eventually asked for it back because I just couldn't deal with the idea of one steady girlfriend. That was the end of formally going steady, but I continued to have warm feelings for Amanda, and from time to time we would get together—even during college and afterwards—and the serious question we had was whether or not we should ever get married. I really loved her, but, you know, she and I never went to bed together the whole time we were dating. We did almost everything else, but somehow consummating our relationship seemed a sort of sacrilege: if we were ever going to get married we wanted in some weird way to be pure for each other.

In many ways, my own experience was similar. In high school, after my sexual encounter with Eileen, I went steady with a series of girls—with Annabelle, a petite redhead; with Joanne, a football cheerleader whom everyone thought to be a real knockout; and with a number of others whose names and faces I can no longer recall. All of these relationships were sexual up to a certain point, and then we would be careful about continuing our pleasure. This was especially true with Joanne—the first of many I considered as an eventual marriage partner. Beautiful Joanne was a fierce guardian of her virginity and every time we were on the couch at her parents' house or together in the back seat of my car she would allow me to play with her while she would play with me, and then we would rub up against each other fully clothed, "dry humping" (as we called it then) for dear life. When I reached orgasm it was always into my own underwear, an event which aroused my mother's curiosity as she attempted to understand how the shorts I had put in the laundry could be so stained. "It's a sweat stain or something, Mom," I would say. "I was playing football the other day, and I must have gotten my clothes all sweated up."

In college, as well, I continued to distinguish between the marriageable girl and the sexual partner. Shortly after the collegiate episode and resulting fright about Peggy Sue's possible pregnancy, I became involved with Rachel, the woman I was eventually to marry. Because of fears engendered by my near escape with Peggy Sue, and a resolve to bring "order" and "respectability" to my life, I could not bring myself fully to make love with Rachel for nearly a year although we saw each other steadily and we eventually even lived together. I encouraged her to be the epitome of the "nice girl" and made few sexual demands upon her, while I threw myself into my studies, redirecting my erotic energies from physical closeness to academic accomplishment. In many respects this solution only continued a tendency already in force; as I had in high school, I again began to flee from sexuality when it seemed that sex would afford my partner a claim to my time and to my inmost self. It was only when Rachel and I had decided to marry that we had full sexual relations. Such mutual deprivation, as I later learned, was not exactly the best foundation on which to build a marriage.

Today such ritual abstinance no longer prevails to the degree that it did only a decade or two ago. The distinction between the female as "good" or as "available for sex" has largely broken down. Adolescents, both female and male, now become aware of sex and contraception much earlier, and they are learning to treat sex as a means of self-expression rather than as a forbidden secret. Still, for those of us who grew to maturity in the fifties and sixties, ambivalent feelings about sexuality remain. Despite the arrival of a sexual revolution, I assume that this ambivalence continues to affect young people. The legacy of the double standard was the foundation on which we built our initial relationships, and this code remains part of our inheritance. As men, we want to be cared for by women (in the ways that our mothers once cared for us), but we also want to dominate women (as we often sought to dominate the sexual partners of our youth). At the same time, many of us seek to share in relationships based on a commitment to equality—or at least we claim to do this. The images and expectations of the past return again to haunt the present, and the bitter experiences of failed marriages and lost relationships have taught many of us that our training in one world did not prepare us for life in another.

Notes

1. For a discussion of these questions, see Nancy Chodorow, *The Reproduction of Mothering: Psychoanalysis and the Sociology of Gender* (Berkeley and Los Angeles: University of California Press, 1978), and Dorothy Dinnerstein, *The Mermaid and the Minotaur* (New York: Harper and Row, 1977).
2. Nancy Chodorow, *The Reproduction of Mothering,* pp. 7, 106–108.
3. Mirra Komarovsky, *Dilemmas of Masculinity: A Study of College Youth* (New York. Norton, 1976), chapter 9.

CHAPTER 4

Rachel: Scenes From A First Marriage

"First marriages are like transitional objects."
—TOM FOGARTY—*Psychotherapist, in conversation*

"Ted, I'm leaving you."
"What?"
"I'm suffocating here."
"You're what?"
"I said—I'm leaving you."
"I don't understand."
"I guess you don't. I'll start again. Ted, I'm leaving you. Do you get it now?"
"Is this some kind of joke?"
"Hah, hah."
"Joanna?"
"The marriage is over."
"I don't believe this."
"Why don't you start believing it?"
—AVERY CORMAN, *Kramer vs. Kramer*

The ambivalent feelings of contemporary men are mirrored more dramatically in our relationships with women than in any other aspect of our lives. We want women who will take care of us and women who will stand on their own feet, women who are lovers, women who are achievers, and women who are mothers. Although we may want women who are competent and strong, we also want women who are dependent and submissive. We want women who have minds of their own, but who will do our bidding. This is clearly a contradictory and confusing set of desires, and it can seriously undermine our relationships and marriages. A main task toward becoming a secure adult male today is to clarify our expectations about women and to develop new and more realistic ways to relate to them. Only then can we free ourselves from outworn needs and from the clash between past roles and present realities.

In my marriage to Rachel, a marriage that ended bitterly in divorce, I attempted to adopt traditional lessons about the roles of men and women and to learn from newer and more egalitarian models of male and female behavior. Rachel, for her part, was similarly caught between old ways and new, a dilemma she sought to resolve by means of the women's movement during the heady, early days of contemporary feminism at the beginning of the nineteen-seventies. The result of our struggles—those we fought inside ourselves as well as with each other—was pain, conflict and the end of our marriage. Seen in a more positive way, this ending led to self-knowledge and an ability to form new relationships on a firmer, more intentional basis.

In the beginning, Rachel and I came together out of needs which we did not clearly perceive and did not understand. Recoiling from a sexuality that was freer and more dangerous than I wanted, I sought a traditional, safe, and permanent relationship. I wanted a woman who would take care of me and yet mainly to be subordinate and dependent. I think that Rachel, for her part, looked for protection in our marriage—the protection of a man who seemed similar to her own father, but who was not yet the adult equivalent of her father and against whom she might contend when necessary. These diverse feelings gave birth to our mutual love and dependence; but they also produced our underlying resistance to each other. Eventually a growing urge to free ourselves from the longings which had brought us together helped to end our marriage.

Our two families had exerted sometimes subtle and sometimes overt pressure on us to marry. Their reason for this, I think, was a wish for us to reproduce and to validate the choices that they, themselves, had made: to marry early, to "settle down" and to raise children. As I look back, such familial urging does not seem to have been altogether wrong. Given a traditional perspective, such advice was wise. It was a wisdom that applied when roles and relationships were relatively fixed and when the nuclear, male-headed household was the most important foundation of life, work, and social position. Our parents had chosen their mates early; they had remained together; they had raised families; they had "grown together" and ultimately, they had prospered. They now assured Rachel and me that we, too, could find stability and could repeat some of those experiences. The trouble was that she and I had grown up in a rapidly changing world with expectations about ourselves and about relationships which had begun to differ seriously from those of our parents.

After we had lived together during my senior year of college, I left Rachel to move across the country to begin my graduate studies. Besides being necessary to my future career, the move—as I now discover—was part of a last effort to free myself from desires for easy stability and from parental expectations that I begin to settle down. My enjoyment of a sense of freedom was short-lived, however. Although I saw many women and began to establish new relationships, my attachment to Rachel and the kind of security she represented seemed to prevail. My parents helped contribute to this. At one point, as I recall, my family got wind that I was sowing some wild oats. My father showed up unexpectedly to discuss my recent life and to urge me to consider marriage to Rachel. By that time, I did not need much serious arm twisting, for I actually had begun to feel frightened by the wide range of choices which relationships with a number of new women presented. I missed Rachel, and especially the care and understanding she offered.

Soon afterward, Rachel and I had a large and ornate wedding. Looking now at the carefully posed, glossy photographs of this event, it is apparent that Rachel and I did not merely marry each other; our two families had become linked as well. That day, all of us affirmed a traditional idea of marriage, based on clearly defined roles and undisturbed by less orthodox paths to growth and fulfillment. I remember the panic that seized me a moment before the ceremony began. I broke out in a cold sweat, which began to wilt my starched shirt-front. "What am I doing here?" I asked my brother who was to act as best man. "I'm only 22, and I haven't lived enough or had enough experience to get married yet."

"Man, if you haven't worked that out," he said, "It's too late now!"

In the first years of our marriage, Rachel and I followed a path that made us face a variety of contradictory feelings. On the surface we had what might seem a fairly traditional marriage, which we attempted to portray as a model of harmony and perfection. I earned the major portion of our upkeep in my first job as a young university lecturer. Although Rachel worked to supplement our income, it was clear that my job and my career were central and that they gave shape and definition to our marriage. Moreover, I felt little responsibility for the daily chores such as house cleaning, washing dishes, or shopping. Although I occasionally ran a vacuum cleaner around the floor or went to the market for groceries, these were by definition not a man's obligation, and certainly not that of a married man who was the main family breadwinner.

That our marriage had assumed this structure was a rather odd development. When Rachel and I had lived together in college, we had shared equally in the household chores. Both of us were occupied with school, and if there was work to be done around the apartment, then whoever was available could damn well do it. Moreover, in those days Rachel and I were at the same level of schooling and held similar views about work goals. She had, in fact, done better than I in several courses. We had earned our undergraduate degrees, and she wanted to begin her own graduate studies. The marriage somehow turned a relationship of rough equality into one of assigned sex roles and inequality.

Other dilemmas made our life together more difficult. Although we had begun to diverge from some of the patterns transmitted to us by our families, we retained others. We could not, for example, confront each other very directly with a clear expression of our needs or attitudes, for neither of us had ever learned to do this. Thus, we transmitted indirect messages. In a pinch I could always rely on my anger to get my needs met, and I could attempt to overwhelm her with my masculine superiority; or I could throw up my hands and claim that the world was just too hard, inviting her to take care of me and to set things right just as a mother would for a child. Rachel, for her part, could often count on an outburst of her own rage to get me to respond to her wishes. She could also rely on cajolery and could cleverly analyze the situation to get an intended response; or, if all else failed, she could retreat into feminine dependency. She could invite me to become her father or caretaker in the same way I could invite her to become my mother. And so we went around and around, constrained by old messages and family histories, and caught within traditional sex roles by which men and women have been confined. Without the ability to comprehend our situation or the sources of our conflict, we were often at loggerheads with each other and with the best parts of ourselves, as well.

I found too, that working at my first professional job consumed much of my time and energy. I suspect that this would have been the case whether I worked in college teaching, in another profession, or in business. Writers about the stages of adult life tell us that the twenties are a period of acute struggle, both internal as well as in relation to the outside world. Gail Sheehy calls this the "Trying Twenties,"[1] and Daniel Levinson labels it a time of "Early Adult Transition."[2] It is a phase through which men (and increasingly women) seek to enter the adult world by establishing a career, finding a teacher or mentor, and, in Levinson's words, "building a first provisional life structure."[3]

I had my doctoral thesis to finish, classes to prepare, a first book to complete, and senior faculty to impress with my ambition and dedication. I attached myself to a series of advisors and older colleagues who seemed ready to help an earnest young man. I thought about my work constantly, and I bit my fingernails nearly to the roots. All of this left little time for Rachel and me to share. Ironically, when we moved to a cottage far out of town in order, I think, to preserve some small living space for ourselves, the commute to the city consumed much remaining time. "A man in his twenties," Sheehy aptly notes, "must funnel his energies into making an independent way in the world or else be ridiculed. . . . [This is] the time to earn the credentials that will win him approval from others and rewards from society. If he burns with desire to gain recognition as well, a man must be faithful and endlessly attentive to his real loved one: the career."[4]

Matters eventually reached a head when, after a few years of marriage, Rachel and I decided to have a child. Such a decision, after all, was part of the unspoken program our families had laid out for us and part also of our own expectations and those of the wider world. For Rachel and me, pregnancy was a time of growing expectation, but also of growing apprehension. We both wanted a child, but she wondered how motherhood would affect her residual aspirations for a career, and I wondered whether child rearing would cut appreciably into the energy I could mobilize for my job. Who would take care of this baby? How much time would we have left to give to each other? How much would I have to share in the diapering and the feeding? Surviving in the competitive arena of work was difficult enough. What more must I sacrifice for this new life that we were bringing into the world? Unfortunately, despite our anxiety, we did not discuss most of these concerns with each other.

Rachel and I did participate, however, in childbirth classes and in a Lamaze "natural" birth at a time when such a process was relatively novel. Jacob's birth was perhaps the most committed and intense moment that she and I would have together (as it must be for most couples who share in such an experience). Throughout the delivery I paced her in her breathing exercises, panting and blowing along as she worked to bring Jake into the world. "It's a boy!" we both joyfully yelled moments after he emerged from the womb. "It's your baby, too," Rachel said to me with a sigh of satisfaction as she held him close just after the birth. "I know, honey," I replied. "I love you, Rachel, and I love him too."

Love, sadly, was not enough. The added daily pressures of having a child heightened the problems in our relationship. Although Rachel and I at times fought about our differences and about the conflicts that we felt, we were not readily able to talk about either the fights or the conflicts. After all, our marriage (for outside consumption) approached perfection. Our families seemingly expected it to be so, and we attempted to display the same aura of contentment to our friends. In a "perfect" relationship, how could one talk about feelings of anger, resentment, and sadness? Both Rachel and I were deceived by the illusion that we shared our feelings honestly while, in fact, we were not really able to touch each other or to explain our needs and concerns.

As is so often the case, our stifled feelings returned with a vengeance. My inner experience told me that I did not actually live in a "perfect" union, and I became more angry and disagreeable as time went on. I began to pick fights with Rachel over minor issues and I increasingly shut myself off from friends and the rest of the world. Eventually, I refused for the most part to talk with anyone on the telephone, considering such communication a potential drain on my energy and an intrusion into my carefully scheduled work time. I began to run six to eight miles a day (although oddly I never saw this as affecting my time or energy), and I became an increasingly strict vegetarian. This behavior was obviously an indirect way of giving voice to the emotions which I could not allow myself to express directly. It also allowed me to escape somewhat from the pain and frustration which I felt in this less-than-perfect marriage.

Rachel and I began to clash especially over the question of how to apportion our time so that we shared child-care and house-care duties. At first I refused to acknowledge that I had an obligation to participate equally in Jake's care. After all, it was a man's place to pursue a career and earn the major income, and that of a woman to provide support for children and the household. This was the way the world had always been, and even if I believed intellectually that some changes were probably overdue, I could not make my emotions square with my beliefs.

After much conflict, I was finally able to acknowledge that, indeed, Rachel had a right equal to mine to pursue her career training and other interests and that I should take on more domestic duties. Nonetheless, we never ceased to snipe at each other over the daily allotment of time for personal or collective needs; our wrangling intensified and our mutual resentment grew.

I have found in subsequent conversations with men that a just division of time and labor looms as a fundamental issue in many lives and relationships. On the surface this seems a simple problem. Children need to be cared for, dishes need to be washed, floors swept, income earned, and there must be something left for personal pursuits and for time to be together. Indeed, many contemporary men now feel an obligation to share in house responsibilities. But the questions remain regarding how much men are really willing to do and how the experience of sharing fits with their own sense of what it means to be a man. Although other men might not experience the same persistent struggles that I had with Rachel, an underlying conflict remains between old lessons and new expectations.

"This is a difficult time to be a man," notes Jim, an academic in his mid-thirties. "The expectations of manhood are less clear than they used to be. It feels like *more* is expected of us at work and at home. I feel a lot of anger over the changes in my life, and yet I find difficulty in directing that anger at anything or anybody: it seems like just the current condition of life. Still, I do often feel resentment at Lois for asking me to change my ways. She puts me on the defensive a lot. I know that on one hand I accept her needs and I acknowledge the kinds of changes in the sharing of house care and child care that she wants. But I find that it's almost impossible for me to meet all of her expectations. I often don't and then she gets pissed, and I get defensive. We yell at each other and much of my resentment comes out over just how we apportion time together: my being late, for example, to get home to take care of the kids is a source of much conflict for both of us."

Jim notes (as do other men) that the dinner hour is an especially difficult time of day. The attempt to share household chores at this busy moment seems to bring out much of the anger and emotion that lurk beneath the surface. "Everything sort of falls apart at dinner time," Jim says. "The kids get really cranky: Lois is trying to get dinner (or else it's my turn to cook), and it would really be helpful if I could get home around five o'clock to help take care of the kids for that last hour. Yet I seem almost unable to do it. I don't know whether I'm just avoiding something I don't want to do (which is what she thinks), or whether (as I claim) I can't do it because I really need that time to myself. The demands on me at work are heavy; they exceed what I possibly can accomplish, and there is no way to pick up the slack, except by staying at my office through the five o'clock hour. I also feel that I sometimes need to jog or do some other kind of exercise to help retain my own sanity. I might, of course, be striking back at Lois for the demands and expectations the family places on me, but I have to say that this doesn't always seem real clear: I usually seem to have a rational explanation for my inability to get home as early as she wants."

"It's so easy for us to get into an adversary relationship over these things," Jim says. "We always seem to be negotiating: 'okay, you can have this, but I've got to keep that'; and it seems as if I have to try to justify almost everything I do. This would somehow be better if I could prove that I was in school writing tomorrow's lecture, but if I don't get home until 5:30 because I was off running, this is totally unacceptable. It's strange to think that this is all ultimately supposed to be good for me and that it will make my marriage closer and things easier for both of us. You know, I really don't think that the strain I feel can be any good for me, but I'm not yet ready to drop the new expectations, either. Having to live with both tradition and change is really hard."

Other men express variations on this theme. Philip, for example, is a magazine editor in a large east coast city. He earns the major share of the family income, while his wife Joanne attends graduate school part-time to earn a professional degree. When he is at home, Phil shares the household chores on what he calls "a more-or-less even basis," but he notes that since Joanne is at home more than he, "she is really the point-person for much of what needs to be done. She organizes our labor, and tells me pretty much what I should do. So you might say that I really don't take a lion's share of responsibility. I let her direct the traffic, so to speak. It's a fairly even division of labor when we are both on the scene, but, of course, she is on the scene more than I am."

"The main thing that Joanne demands of me," Philip says, "is that I be home at a reasonable hour to help with the dinner and getting the kids to bed. I could always find reasons to hang out at my job a little longer, to wrap a few things up, to get ready for tomorrow. But if I'm not home on time, it really brings us into conflict. I'm expected to help in the morning, to get the children off to school or to daycare, but especially in the evening I'm supposed to help with everything that needs to be taken care of."

Phil adds thoughtfully, "I don't know how these changes evolved from the traditional male and female roles. I guess that when Joanne joined a women's support group, she began voicing some new ideas. I was pretty angry about this at first, but I've learned that I genuinely prefer to be around a woman who asserts her own independence. I know that I would be frustrated if I had to stay home like she did at the beginning of our marriage. Joanne has always been a very independent person, and meeting other women and reading women's literature helped to crystallize her ideas. I really think, though, that she would have made changes in her life *despite* the climate of the times—*whenever* she might have felt upset by how she was living."

"I feel guilty," Philip notes, "that Joanne and I don't actually divide things with complete equality. If she asks for a 50-50 split in time and work, I really don't think I could find a logical argument against it. Just because I'm a man doesn't mean that I'm more inherently privileged than she is, but such a request would put me in a dilemma. On one hand, I feel that our sharing should ideally be equal. On the other hand, I don't see how I could give up my full-time career for such an equally shared relationship."

As did Jim, Philip expresses frustration: "I find this all tremendously hard. When I'm at work, I really put in long hours. I come home and I'm tired, and tense. I've been through rush-hour traffic, and I have my own needs. When I walk in the door all I want is to kick off my shoes, sit down, and maybe then take a shower and have a drink. But what I actually have to do is to take care of two kids, and for the next few hours I don't really get a chance to relax. Joanne now stays home one full day a week and on that Monday night when I come home, she says, 'Okay, Buddy, take over; I've been with the kids all day long and now it's your turn,' and then she goes and relaxes in the bath tub." Phil goes on to say in a louder voice: "This really makes me angry. I really don't think it's fair, and I bitch and complain." But then more reflectively, he notes, "In a sense, I don't have much of a case. I've been privileged to be able to go into town and have a chance to do some creative work. And you know, I really feel confused over this because Joanne has been running around after a 14-month-old infant for a whole day, and she does definitely need some relief. But I need some relief too, dammit! The question is how much guilt should I have for leaving her at home? I've worked hard, but at the same time, I have a basically satisfying and creative job despite all the turmoil that it entails. I'm tired, but I've had an opportunity that Joanne hasn't. Should I feel guilty for this? Should I be angry? Who is going to pick up the slack if I don't? You know, I really have to say that this is a very confusing situation."

As in the above case of Philip and Joanne, Rachel and I opened a new phase in our relationship when she joined a women's support group and began discussing her feelings in a feminist context. For Rachel, the initial question was how to deal with becoming a mother and the change in personal expectations that this entailed. At the time—during the late sixties and early seventies—it was not yet generally accepted (strange as it might seem) that women could, as a matter of course, combine marriage and child rearing with the demands of a profession. Rachel and the women in her group struggled with this issue and with years of conditioning which dictated that having children meant a retreat from the active world and confinement essentially to homemaking and support for a husband. These discussions also touched on the nature of her relationship with me and that of other women with their men. Increasingly, Rachel made it clear that what she wanted was a situation of precise equality in which we would carefully divide the daily tasks to be done at home and the time spent in child care. Despite my resentment and fear, I slowly acceded to the needs that she now expressed.

Even though I began to acknowledge Rachel's wishes, I was not fully in support of the new order, and I expressed my resistance and ambivalence in a variety of ways. Even though I could recognize on an intellectual level the justice of Rachel's position (and that of women in general), I could not make my emotions and feelings coincide. I had been raised to believe that men were superior, that women would automatically take care of us, and that we could expect them to be passive and receptive. I had learned this in my childhood, in my teenage years, in playing the dating game, and in my experience with male friends. Now I was expected to shift gears and to put aside my own pressing needs. I was called on to think of myself as no more privileged than my wife or her friends, as not entitled to special consideration or care. Although I sensed that the changes Rachel encouraged were probably necessary, the nature of her feelings—and what I took to be the stridency with which she expressed them—seemed a great threat to me as a person and as a man.

I felt particularly threatened when Rachel wanted to make changes in the quality of our intimacy and in our lovemaking. After one of her group meetings, she told me that I had never really given her sexual pleasure and that I did not adequately postpone my own orgasms so that she could enjoy the act of love. I was hurt and surprised to hear this, but I had to admit that I did not delay my orgasms very well and that I was not very interested in long, drawn-out foreplay of the kind she said that women needed for maximum pleasure. It might sound naive to admit this, but at the time I did not even know that men could intentionally delay orgasm or that women could achieve climax by prolonged and deliberate clitoral stimulation. Perhaps it was a question of the changing times, perhaps my own ignorance (an ignorance difficult to confess, since I fancied myself an "experienced man"), but I was dumbfounded to hear that Rachel considered me inadequate as a lover and that many of her new women friends felt the same about their own partners.

For several months, Rachel and I worked to bring more pleasure and enjoyment to our lovemaking. For the most part, such responsibilities seemed to rest with me. She seemed to expect me to devise ways to add to her enjoyment while it seemed to me that this meant curtailing my own pleasure. As with the question of dividing our time schedule more equally, I felt a commitment out of fairness and logic to comply with her sexual wishes and needs. However, I also felt hostile and defensive because my male prerogatives were being questioned. Deep inside, I still thought that women should accept their men pretty much as they were, that women should be generally subordinate, and that they should help build up our self-esteem. Being called selfish and egotistical was difficult enough. Being told that we were also inadequate lovers rubbed salt into the wounds.

I was, it seemed, not the only man traversing such difficult terrain. At sessions of my men's group—a group started by several of us whose wives had been meeting together—we shared our mutual dismay and our recipes for change. "Sometimes now in lovemaking," one man disclosed, "my jaws ache when I go down on my wife. The only way she can get off is through oral stimulation, and I feel that it's important to comply with her needs, however long it takes." We all felt attacked in the place where it hurt most. It seemed that a shot had been aimed by our partners not merely at our precious male egos, but at our balls, as well. We felt that we had been made to pay for the easy assumptions with which we grew up and for the feelings of superiority shared by all previous generations of men. Try as I might, I felt I could not learn the new lessons quickly or thoroughly enough. It seemed that I was being called a failure to my face (and probably behind the closed doors of Rachel's group meetings). I began to see myself in those terms, as a man who, under the new rules, could not give women pleasure, and I finally began not really to care. Out of anger and disappointment, I began to resist Rachel's requests, and I acted as if her demands and needs constituted an intolerable burden for me.

In the midst of this dilemma, Rachel and I were asked to appear on a local television station as an example of a couple that was attempting to create a new and equally shared relationship. This was a startling event, the irony of which I could only appreciate somewhat later when Rachel and I were ending our marriage. On television we spoke about how we had worked to change our relationship, and we spoke rather pompously about how other couples might achieve a similar equality. By this time, however, we were scarcely speaking to each other, and most of our exchanges had to do with an elaborate planning of schedules and with wrangling over which of us might be taking the most advantage of the other.

Not long afterwards, we both began to turn to outside partners in the vain hope that an "open" marriage would somehow save our life together. In truth, I was the one who initiated this process. I contrived to have an extramarital affair which I somehow (mainly unconsciously) knew that Rachel would discover and which I guessed would repay her for altering the assumptions with which our marriage had begun. The affair was also an attempt to regain the sense that I was a sexually adequate man and a way to reassert my buried beliefs in the principles of male superiority. At any rate, Rachel quickly discovered my transgressions, and she eventually repaid me in kind. Even when that occurred, and when we both agreed to see outside partners on a regular basis, I still could not bring myself to acknowledge that Rachel had an equal right to act as I had done. Somehow, my belief in a moral double-standard prevailed, and I was shocked that Rachel would actually betray me as I had betrayed her.

When these events took place, the ending of our marriage was only a matter of time. From a couple which had seemed to exemplify some of the attempts to construct new relationships between men and women, we had become a pair married only in name. Finally, Rachel and I separated with the same sort of recrimination and anger which has attended so many marital breakups during the last decade.

Long after the ending of my marriage, I continued to blame the women's movement and the new feminism for the struggle through which I had passed. Later, I came to see that such resentment and hostility were not entirely justified. The women's movement, it is true, confronted me and a generation of men with a need to re-think the roles and assumptions of our youth. Such a re-evaluation has been painful, and many of us are still resisting change at the very time that we intellectually advocate a basic shift in values. Men today are divided, within themselves and in their public attitudes and actions, and the split is most profound in relation to women and the feminist movement. Many of us will agree that contemporary feminism has widened the range of possible male behaviors and has freed us from slavish conformity to tradition. Many of us will acknowledge that feminism has made our dealings with both men and women more open and egalitarian. Yet, we often remain confused and divided in our response to feminism and in our reactions to the needs of women to be treated as equals and as partners. Indeed, many of us reveal our ambivalence in statements about the women's movement which in the same conversation—and almost within the same breath—might range from anger and resentment to gratitude and respect.

"The women's movement had a big impact on me in terms of helping me see other people as just human beings," Larry, a mental-health worker, says. "At first, I really didn't give much thought to it. I wasn't very political and for a time I just pooh-poohed these ideas. Then as I thought and read more about it, I could understand that I had always felt the ways that women said they did: that I had felt left out of things a good bit of the time and without any real power." Even though Larry is well over six feet tall and radiates both confidence and physical strength, he says that in his youth he was "a kind of a withdrawn anxious kid who never really felt 'with' what was going on, and for that reason I felt that I could not be a real man and be appreciated for what I was." Odd as it may seem, he says, "this kind of experience made it easier for me to understand what women must have gone through in their own lives and how they felt deprived of real identity and power." Larry continues:

> I think that the real beginning of my own understanding of women and what they felt came out of some work I was doing in group therapy. I was able to have some very close relationships with some women in that group without it becoming a question of having sexual closeness. I became more aware of the impact I had on them as a man. I felt that I never really understood women before, and since the women in this group—if not exclusively feminists—still had feminist values, I came to accept these values because I saw them connected to real people and their struggles with the world. I finally understood more of what they wanted for themselves, from relationships, and from their work and careers. And I realized that, after all, these were the same things I was dealing with myself. I felt good about this and it helped me not to play the traditional male role. There were women who could accept the things about me—my feelings—that I always was so afraid to express, and I began to see these women as not merely images and projections of my fantasies but as real live people. I began to realize that I didn't want just to have sexual relationships with women which might have been convenient and easy, but which also happened to be lonely. From this I learned that I really didn't need to keep women out of my emotional world, and that I could take risks in real life, since I took risks in that controlled setting.

"In a strange way," says Edward, a young molecular biologist, "the women's movement has allowed men more freedom: it permits us to break out of a narrow model of what a man is supposed to be and gives us license to show our shortcomings and our feelings. It also frees us from having to play the role of 'protector' which society previously expected."

"In looking at old nineteen-fifties and nineteen-sixties movies," Edward adds, "it's surprising to see the kinds of expectations that existed for men and women. It's appalling how badly women were treated then and what was asked of men: to be dominant and in control all the time, and unemotional. Men had to land on both feet, even if they looked ridiculous in the process. In a way, the women's movement has shown us that it was all right not to be in control all the time and that one could also be a little dependent for a change."

But Edward expresses some less positive feelings, as well. "Initially," he says, "I had to accept the fact that women were right in much of their criticism of men and that a lot of their anger was understandable and fair. I wanted to change in order to respond to the criticism of the women I was with, but then it got to the point that one began to realize that even with these changes women would continue to complain, attack, and criticize, and finally one had to say 'screw this!' I've changed my actions and feelings, but still it doesn't seem enough. I finally came to realize that not everything is wrong with what I used to do—for example, taking the lead and initiating relationships. Just because women might not feel comfortable with these things—or if they realize that they are not particularly good at something because you have been doing it all your life—why, that's still okay and nothing to be ashamed of. I finally have come to see that it is really good to be a man—to be male—and I'm not just speaking as an antifeminist reactionary when I say this, but I think that at some point it just has to be said."

Some men speak about their anger at the women's movement as an agent in the breakup of their marriages or love relationships, an anger which bears upon my own experience. Jim, for instance, confesses his conviction that, "the women's movement led directly to the end of my first marriage. My wife was involved with a women's collective in the west coast city where we lived during the mid-seventies, and the women in that group put a lot of stress on separatism, on the need for women finally to live alone from men. The scene there went beyond any rational critique of couples' living arrangements, and I finally found myself in a situation where I was viewed as 'the enemy' despite anything that I actually did. To the women in her group I was considered an antagonist merely because I was a man, and because my wife and I maintained a relationship together. And the longer this continued, the more difficult it was for us to live together and to work out our lives in a mutual way. Finally I just wasn't willing anymore to be cast as the heavy or to share her with the women in her group, and we each had to go our separate ways. But I have to say that I still feel a lot of resentment about how we ended and also a sense that I was not fairly used."

Jack, a financial consultant, cites a somewhat different example. He and Pat, the woman with whom he had been living, separated not so much because the women's movement constituted a threat to their relationship as because they each seemed to have interpreted the new rules in different ways. "I think that I was supportive of Pat's career and her desire to be accepted on her own terms," Jack said. "I've come to believe that all people have certain needs, and if she wanted to go to graduate school or to have professional work, then I had to give her support for that. In general, I've come to feel that all adult people should be able to work and support themselves; that men and women both have skills and talents which they should be able to develop. The time came, however, when Pat decided that she didn't want to pursue her career immediately and that she needed time off to develop the emotional side of herself. I found myself feeling angry when she told me that she didn't want to work for awhile in order to concentrate on her own personal development," Jack explains. "I had come to believe so strongly in the lessons of the women's movement and especially that everyone should be able to have a career, that I became really angry when Pat told me that she wanted to do something else. It seemed to me that Pat had talked all along about feminist rights and the need to get a professional education and then suddenly she decided in the name of her growth as a person and a woman that she didn't want to have a job. That just didn't seem fair and it left me confused about my own values and the meaning of her feminist beliefs. It was, I think, one of the important sources of conflict which led eventually to the end of our relationship."

Such divided feelings, however, often mask a process of growth, a process which helps us to resolve our contradictory desire that women should be subordinate and dependent while they are also self-sufficient and strong. Much of this involves not only learning to sympathize with the feelings and views which women express, but also attempting to be clearer and more definite about our own needs and the ways in which we can provide for them. Often this can only happen in a new relationship, as we outgrow the patterns of the past. Such was the case, for example in the ending of my marriage with Rachel and in my subsequent relationship with Sara. I resolved that from the very beginning of a connection with a new person, I would work to make my motives and feelings clear, and that I would not rely so much on the opinions and dictates of the outside world as to what constituted a "good" or acceptable relationship. I have not abandoned or rejected the lessons

I learned from the women's movement—lessons about how men can share with women both emotionally and materially. Instead, I have tried to build on those lessons and to apply them more consciously. Today, I should note that Rachel and I better understand the responsibility we each bore for ending our marriage, and we are much less willing to attribute its dissolution to the workings of feminism: for her part feminism as a "liberating" force, and for me, as a sinister agent of unhappiness. If there is a lesson in this, it is to accept one's own past without casting blame, to learn from experience without becoming its victim.

Notes

1. Gail Sheehy, *Passages: Predictable Crises of Adult Life* (New York: E.P. Dutton, 1976), pp. 83ff.
2. Daniel Levinson, *et al.*, *The Seasons of A Man's Life* (New York: Knopf, 1978), pp. 72ff.
3. *Ibid.*, p. 72.
4. Sheehy, *Passages*, p. 108.

CHAPTER 5

Sara: Beginning Again

8 De Septiembre
Hoy, este día fue una copa plena,
hoy, este día fue la inmensa ola,
hoy, fue toda la tierra.

. . . Entre tú y yo se abrió una nueva puerta
y alguin, sin rostro aún
allí nos esperba.

September 8th
Today, this day was a brimming cup,
today, this day was the immense wave,
today, it was all the earth.

. . . Between you and me a new door opened
and someone, still faceless,
was waiting for us there.

—Pablo Neruda

By the time Rachel and I broke up, I had come to see myself as a less than adequate man. After all, my wife had not been satisfied with me emotionally or through our lovemaking, and I had tried and failed to keep my marriage together. Feelings of incompetence and inadequacy are typical when marriages end. They are, in fact, an important source of the turmoil and pain which accompany divorce.[1] Once before in my life, during my college episode with Peggy Sue, I had felt such doubts about my ability to fulfill the expected masculine roles. Now, however, my sense of doubt and failure was greater. I was faced with both the loss of wife and family and with the loss of a part of my self-conception as a man and as a sexual being. A belief in one's sexual prowess, as sex researcher Bernie Zilbergeld notes in a recent study, constitutes perhaps the core of the male stereotype and the male myth.[2] We all want to believe that we are powerful and desirable lovers, and that sex for us and for our partners is easy, satisfying, and fun.

My doubts about my own abilities and about what it meant to be a man continued for some time after my marriage had fallen apart. The eventual result was not so much a reassertion of the traditional male myth as it was an effort to rethink that myth and not to succumb to it as easily as before. To overcome my doubt and fear, I initially chose a path different from that of my college years. Instead of withdrawing from sexual activity as I had then, I sought many partners as if to prove that Rachel had been wrong, and that I was still a desirable and accomplished mate. Before becoming intimate with someone new, I would often warn her that I tended to reach orgasm quickly and that she would probably not find me as enjoyable and considerate as she might hope. But this, oddly enough, did not seem to deter many. The new women in my life seemed to understand and were willing to make allowances. In reality, however, I do not think that many allowances needed to be made. By trying hard to prove myself as a man who could give pleasure to women, I think that I was able to provide that pleasure. I cannot recall that any of the women with whom I became intimate told me that I had not lived up to her expectations.

In a way, this success became a problem in itself. I put so much emphasis on meeting what I thought were the expectations of women that the whole question of "performance" became divorced from love and enjoyment. Instead of sex as a satisfying addition to the intimacy of two people who cared for each other, it became a chore—a way to prove myself. For a time, I moved as rapidly as I could from partner to partner, acting like the typical newly-separated person seeking to discover myself with a variety of lovers and one-night stands. After a series of such liaisons, when I had been with a new woman literally every night for one hectic week, I felt that I could go no further. I seemed to have proven to myself that I was a virile and desirable man, and I began to wonder about the purpose of my almost mechanical activity. Surely, there was more to love and lovemaking than just physical action and mutual release. Out of my emotional exhaustion and my new experience grew a concern about how other men felt about the requirements that the changing world seemed to place on us. Out of that experience, as well, came a resolve to be more careful about future relationships and a readiness to risk a long-term involvement with someone new.

Sara, however, was not exactly someone new. She had been a teacher at Jake's school, and she and I had silently been attracted to each other during the last years of my marriage to Rachel. We never, thank goodness, had acted on that attraction, but there were times when opportunities had been available. I remember especially a moment on a hot summer's day when Sara and I talked together through the screen door of my house which I kept tightly shut in order to ward off temptation. She had come over to return something that she had borrowed, and, rather than invite her into the house (Rachel and Jake were out of town for a few days), I kept her waiting out on the porch. "Why doesn't he ask me in for a beer," she thought. "I don't dare ask her in," I secretly responded. "I feel a real longing for her and who could tell what might happen. . . ."

Almost two years later, fresh from my marital breakup and time of sexual gymnastics, I finally called Sara for a date. She thought at first that I wanted to talk about my separation and about how it had affected Jacob, but I just wanted to see her and possibly to start where my fantasies had left off on that summer day. As I waited nervously for her to arrive at the "Autumn Equinox," the bar where we were to meet, I wondered whether things would work out or whether Sara would reject me in the way that Rachel had done. Suddenly, I saw her coming through the door, tall and lovely, and moving in her direct and unhesitating manner toward my table. Then a rather odd thing happened: instead of just saying hello, she reached over and kissed my hand. Sara, it seemed, was as nervous as I. Unable to think of what might be appropriate, and yet wanting to show affection, a kiss on the hand was all she could manage. We sat at a corner table and ate and drank until nearly closing time, talking about the past, about our loves and losses, and about the feelings we long had secretly harbored for each other. Then, abruptly moved by our newly discovered affection, we drew close and kissed deeply, most likely to the shock and surprise of everyone still left in the place.

That was the beginning of a whirlwind process by which the two of us became lovers almost too quickly. We were together constantly for the first week or so, only separating to go to work or for unavoidable chores. There soon came a time, however, when we decided to sort out our growing intimacy and to examine the basis on which it rested. I was swept off my feet by the possibility of this new relationship, but I also felt the need to maintain my distance in order to give some shape and regularity to my condition as a separated man. Fortunately, unlike many post-separation men, I was able to slow the process by which Sara and I came together (as she was, as well). After our initial burst of excitement, we began gradually to try to make some sense of our feelings. This, in itself, was something new for me. She was already a "liberated" woman who had assimilated the lessons of the women's movement and had been an independent person. She knew what she wanted in a love relationship, while I was only beginning to learn this myself.

I believe that the start of a relationship sets the course for its entire history. In drawing close to Sara I was partly haunted by memories of my past. I wanted her to take care of me and to administer to my needs, much as I had expected such solicitude from Rachel and, earlier still, from my mother. At the same time, I resisted these atavistic wishes and struggled to learn the lessons of my failed marriage. I began to try to stand on my own feet by caring for my own needs, while asking Sara for her help when I really needed it. She and I worked hard to find a balance between closeness and independence. We developed a pattern in which we would draw near but within which we could reassert our own boundaries. Yet I cannot say that I have ever mastered this process. Maintaining a distinction between intimacy and dependence is a continuing task, one which neither she nor I have completely solved to this day.

Other men have spoken to me about similar experiences in trying to form relationships based on new assumptions.

"Amy and I have a deep love for each other," Stan says. "We came together in an exciting way, a mixture of sexual intrigue and of sharing—our philosophies of life, our concern for people, and many of the ways that we feel about ourselves. Unlike my ex-wife, Amy never is overly critical of me or of anyone else and never tries to control me in ways that my ex-wife did. I think that although Amy and I had some difficult times at the beginning, we have the best process of communication and sharing that I have ever experienced with anyone."

As in my own case, feminism and the impact of the women's movement had been a chief issue in Stan's former marriage. "In contrast with my first marriage," Stan says, "feminism is not a political issue that we spend much time discussing. Amy is someone who just shares with me in nearly everything. If she makes twenty bucks and if some need comes up, she'll give me that money, and I'd do the same for her. She also shares a lot of feelings and perceptions about her profession.

It's a kind of equality not based on 'You do this, I'll do that,' but on being ready to share. I teach her how to work on bicycles and on cars, and she's been teaching me to cook and sew. I think that we *live* the equality in this household. It is complementary: we seem always to be taking up the slack for each other."

"I can always count on Amy doing her share," Stan continues, "but she has her own ideas about how to apportion that share. I may have some anguish about needing to do the chores myself, but then I realize that she does her part and that she doesn't slough off on anything. I think that we really do have a democratic division of labor. Amy doesn't let me do all the hard stuff of daily life; we both do that for each other."

Many problems, however, have arisen in Stan's new relationship. It appears that at this point (shortly after beginning together in a serious way), Stan and Amy have had more success in apportioning domestic labor than in confronting and dealing with their feelings. "Although difficult moments have to be expected," Stan says, "starting out together really has been painful. Amy is just not used to making clear anything that she is thinking and in expressing most of her needs and emotions. Man, she really goes through anxiety and turmoil just explaining what she wants and in working it out with me."

"There are moments when Amy doesn't really stand up for herself and when she defers to my judgment," Stan adds. "Possibly it's the legacy of traditional female training. I wonder about this and I ask her to tell me more about what she needs. I don't always want to be the leader in a relationship anymore, and I find that this is something that the women's movement has helped me with: to follow other people and not always to be the dominant one."

The problem, of course, might not be exclusively Amy's. In becoming serious with a new woman, Stan has consciously avoided a person who presents herself as an overt feminist, and he has thus not been able to enjoy many of the advantages of openness and mutuality which feminism has made available. Stan recognizes some of his responsibility for the difficulties arising with Amy. One special problem is devoting time to his children as well as to the new woman in his life, a difficulty often experienced by both men and women who are starting out with a new partner.

"The fact that I have two kids who live part-time with us is rough for Amy and me. The energy that I devote to the kids, and the fact that Amy and I aren't just together with each other tends to bring on conflicts. Although Amy is willing to compromise, she still resents having to share me so much, and I feel angry about her resentment although I try to understand it. Amy has to share me with the kids, with my work, and with my friends. It really seems hard to hold everything together. I think to myself, 'My God, how can this possibly work? How can I give time to everyone and juggle all the pressures in my life?' "

Part of the difficulty for Stan is the risk of further pain that a new relationship can bring if it too fails. "I don't want to be involved in an intimate relationship and just have it break up, and so I try to protect myself by sometimes holding back feelings and emotions. My divorce brought incredible trauma and difficulty, and I don't want it to happen again. I'm really afraid that if Amy and I remain so involved, I'll eventually go through another breakup, even though I understand my own emotions and responses and can prepare for hard times. Right now I'm suspicious about whether women can love me enough and give me enough in an adult relationship, and I wonder whether I can do this for them. I feel that in some ways what I really want is a kind of childish fantasy (and at the same time I feel it as a very deep need): to be loved totally so I know that my partner will always be there and that I don't have to run the risk of being left."

"Finally," Stan says, "I can protect myself by being with a woman who I think will never leave me and also by being somewhat guarded about my own feelings. At times, I find myself holding back from involvement so that I don't have to confront the pain. But, of course, my relationship with Amy actually entails taking the risk of a painful ending, and so I shift between being open with her and withdrawing into myself. I often change from day to day; variability seems for me the essence of this new relationship."

In the beginning, Sara and I experienced difficulties similar to those of Amy and Stan. As I have noted, she and I began to struggle over how we could learn to trust and to grow close in an emotional as well as a physical way. As a first step, we soon adopted a rather rigid time schedule which helped to preserve both our guarded distance and our growing closeness. We carefully segmented the week into those nights spent together and those spent alone. If our love was to succeed, we both thought, then we could not overburden it with too much initial familiarity nor with expectations that we must each be available whenever the other chose.

Despite our intentions, it was not an easy matter to follow such a schedule. At times, I wanted Sara to be with me almost constantly, and I felt resentful when she would not comply with my wishes. Even though I now acknowledged that men and women should balance their time together with time for individual pursuits, I still had deeply buried feelings that my own requirements came first and that Sara should administer to them. Indeed, I have not yet completely discarded such notions, and at times of stress I find myself still demanding that Sara sacrifice her interests and independence to provide for mine. Recently, in fact, I developed a severe case of hives when I contemplated the possibility that for a time she might not be able to fulfill my needs. Although I denied that this debilitating rash was brought on by my anxiety over her unavailability, I knew deep down that somehow it was.

From the outset, Sara and I fought about a variety of things, some petty and some important: who would do the shopping as well as who might relocate to be near the other's place of work. Mainly, these fights were rooted in our fear of surrendering control, and we each resisted the danger of relinquishing autonomy to the other. Although I often worried that such struggles would lead to another breakup, I soon learned that not all fights are destructive. In laying their cards on the table two people can clarify both their anger and their will to find a resolution. This can be an act of love and commitment as well as an act of hostility. Despite our rocky beginnings, Sara and I—through our mutual struggles—came to understand that we shared a love in which both positive sentiments and angry feelings were permitted. During these times we worked to tell each other as much as possible about our perceptions and emotions. There were moments, however, when I could take no further steps in surrendering the memories of my first marriage or when she could no longer reveal new parts of herself or her feelings—when I still confused her with an ex-wife or she mistook me for a judging father. We then found the need to have a session together with two psychotherapists, a man and a woman, skilled in clarifying issues in relationships and in daily life.

At first, I was wary of such a path, since Rachel and I had gotten little but pain from therapy during the bitter end of our marriage. But not all therapeutic experiences are the same. Rachel and I were coming apart; Sara and I were moving together, and herein lay a great difference. After a session with our therapists, we found that we could be more open with each other, that we could begin to overcome the obstacles which had seemed insurmountable, and that we could then go on. During one such session, I began to picture myself as a kind of bandit or outlaw who moved from boulder to boulder hiding from Sara and occasionally taking a shot at her. This image, in fact, coincided with the perception she had had of me over the previous few months; being able to embody our experience in such a metaphor made it easier to realize how we were behaving with one another. This same image recurs today when I feel a need to withdraw from closeness and to defend myself. I can then step back to look at the impact that my actions have on the woman who is my mate. Although I might not recommend such therapy sessions for everyone attempting to build a relationship or marriage, the sessions seem to have worked for Sara and me. The lessons we learned in the super-charged and electric environment of therapy have stayed with us ever since.

As we have seen, a recurring problem in many new relationships is how to move closer to one's partner in a slow but steady way in order to avoid the pitfalls that an immediate clinging together might entail. Jack, a recently divorced writer, told me, for example:

> When my marriage broke up, it seemed reasonable that I would get right into a relationship with Emily, a woman I had known as a friend for a long time. I felt this tremendous pressure building up to prove myself as a good family man who could maintain a steady connection with a woman despite the fact that my marriage had ended. I noticed also that I had begun to compare Emily with my ex-wife. I felt that I was testing her all the time—looking at her body, and judging how articulate she was and the quality of her jokes. I constantly asked myself if this was the woman I wanted to stay with. In other words, I put such an intense burden on the damn relationship that it was nearly unbearable.
>
> Emily felt a lot of strain, too, and she was continually trying to please me. I couldn't sneeze without her offering a handkerchief, and she responded to my needs all the time, needs that I didn't even know I had. She would meet every casual statement of mine with a serious reply, and she poured a tremendous amount of energy into pleasing me. I think that I began to do the same for her. We both felt a lot of anxiety over whether we could be intimate and whether we could make a relationship together. What was on the line, we felt, was potential success in cementing a *Commitment*. So we were always off balance, and things were completely different from the way we had been as friends.
>
> Then, one night we threw a party and everything came to a head. We

went to sleep when all the guests had left, and I suddenly had a dream in which it was very clear that I wouldn't be staying with Emily. I woke in a sweat, and I couldn't go back to bed. I felt the need to wake her and talk. We turned on the lights and spoke for the rest of the night, and I told her that I was feeling completely unsure of how I wanted the relationship to be—even *if* I wanted it to be. I felt that I could deal with the normal kinds of anxieties and neuroses which we both had (or any people would have). But as a result of the dream it was apparent that even the everyday kind of things were too difficult: our attempts to get each other to like our kids from former marriages, the way she would change even her facial expressions to meet my own. I also began to fear that I was now reproducing the kind of relationship that I had had with my ex-wife, that I tended to stifle and overwhelm the women I was with and didn't give them a chance to be themselves. Emily and I talked about these things, and we were very straight with each other. I said that I couldn't have any commitment to her, that such a strong commitment at the beginning was just crazy. We were both very sad, and we held each other and cried. Later on, it became clear that she didn't want such a strong connection with me but had gotten into a situation where she had been nursing me through the hurt of my failed marriage by trying to anticipate my feelings and to protect me from them.

Emily and I had moved together too fast, and we had no means for dealing with the inevitable issues of needing to know each other as real people. It had become an unrealistic relationship and we finally had to break it off. After that night I wasn't sure whether I was ever going to see her again, and certainly not as a lover. Well, a couple of weeks later we happened to meet by chance and by that time most of our initial tensions and anxieties had evaporated. Something had changed. We both felt a lot of pressure about whether our relationship would last, and now that it seemed to be over, we could again begin to see one another as individuals and not as idealized images. We both realized that we each had problems developing intimacy, and that we had both sabotaged our chance together. Ironically, it seems that we needed to move apart and to start again in a measured and steady way if our feelings for each other would ever have room to grow. Right now, in fact, I don't know what will happen. We see each other rather steadily but without the tension of having to make it work and without the need to be ideal lovers. I feel especially that I had to give up the image of myself as the strong family man who could merely replace one family with another, one central woman in my life with another. It's been a slow, continuous process of self-discovery and even of maturing. In my forties, I think that I've finally begun to grow up, and that I need not define myself through my relationship with a woman and my idealized image of that relationship. I feel, in other words, that this has been a process not only of losing family and love, but of gaining a new part of myself.

In a similar manner, Ted Morgan tells me about his experience in becoming intimate with someone new. Ted is now seeing Jane, a recently divorced woman who has two children and a well-established professional career. "Jane and I go back and forth about our relationship, and at least once a week one of us gets real frightened by the intensity of our bond," Ted says. "I feel that I've jumped into this situation at an astonishing rate, and that I'm holding back very little, but at the very least I've got to try to preserve my own identity. She and I face some real problems together: the pain of her divorce, the question of the kids, my own wariness of involvement. But I have to say that I'm really attracted to Jane because she knows what she wants, she knows who she is, she's a very hot-shit woman and is challenging to be with. I've always got to be on my toes and to put out a high level of energy. More than any woman I've ever known, Jane demands self-awareness and engagement. She stands her own ground and I'd much rather be stimulated by someone who has their own ideas and their own preferences than to be with somebody who just says 'me, too.' And I guess that ultimately to have this kind of experience I have to take the whole package, kids and all, but it's a very *big* package."

The role of children in a new relationship is a formidable issue for Ted, as for many other men. "The problem with the kids," Ted says, "is that suddenly I'm faced with inheriting two of someone else's children and with having to figure out how to be with them. It's a real double whammy: not only a new relationship, but new kids as well. I would like to reach some kind of resolution as we go along, because if Jane and I just ignore this problem and then try later to deal the kids in, and it doesn't work, things are going to be just horrible for all of us. I think that Jane and I will have to confront the question of how much time we spend together and how much with the kids, and spending time with children is not the same as just being alone with her. This is entirely different from how I related to women in the past. Then it was just two people and we had plenty of time together. I guess that ultimately I don't really know if I can share Jane or anybody with a bunch of kids."

"Even without the kids," Ted says, "Jane and I battle over who controls the time together and the time apart. It's easy just to get lost in her and in her intensity and in our need to be together. I find it important, however, to have some time and space to remember who I am so I can bring my own self to the relationship and not be swallowed by it. I maintain my own apartment, and I can't see myself giving up that sort of independence in the near future. Our situation is so complex and has gone so fast that I just need that place as my refuge. I even find myself being resentful when Jane wants to see me every night. It seems that all sorts of things are happening with so many people: Jane and I, her kids, her ex-husband, my ex-women friends. There's a whole web of human dynamics that we constantly need to contend with. I sometimes feel that, in becoming involved, Jane and I took two giant steps forward and that it's now time to step back."

"I know," Ted concludes, "that in a relationship you make compromises and give things up, and that you also get a lot. What you get when things are good is ultimately worth everything that you have to surrender. In a relationship you have to renounce quite a bit and to compromise—about who makes dinner, about when you go to bed, about who walks the dog—and this is to be expected. But the changes that I envision as Jane and I move closer together seem so big. My network of friends and my time alone is really important, and I don't know if I can give them up. I'm involved now because I'm tempted by the goodies. The time is coming, however, when we'll have to decide if we'll share the bulk of our lives together, and this also involves two little bulks—Jane's kids. I know that women do this all the time for men—they become stepmothers to men's children—but men are just beginning to learn to take on such responsibilities, both emotionally and materially. Are we to be fathers? Stepfathers? Guys who get up and leave in the morning? Right now I have no intelligent model of what this should be like. I'm willing to suspend disbelief for awhile and to try it out, but I don't know what will happen. These new issues are so difficult for everyone involved in them."

After more than a year of contending with the kinds of questions just described, Sara and I decided to live together. Despite the somewhat artificial nature of the schedule which had allowed us to spend some nights with each other and some apart, we had in this way become more used to our commitment, and we had tested the possibilities of making a life with each other. My son Jake, however, found it difficult to accept Sara's presence during the half of the week that he spent with me, and he struggled against being part of this new threesome. There was a day, for example, when we had just moved into a new apartment. Rain poured, boxes and furniture were strewn everywhere, my dog was underfoot, a carpenter worked in the other room building shelves and bookcases, and Jake yelled in frustration at both Sara and me: "Father, I never wanted you to separate from my mother, and now I have to suffer by moving all the time from one house to another and from Rachel to you. . . . I hated Sara when she was my teacher, and I hate her now! And I think that she is no good for you, either!" There was no reasoning with Jake, and finally Ed, the carpenter, hearing the commotion, wandered into the room. "Don't worry, folks," he said in his quiet way, "My two kids now live with my new wife and me, and getting used to each other was really hard at first. And Jake, why don't you try to give Sara and your dad a chance? My own children finally learned to like their stepmother after a time." If Ed's intervention did not completely break the spell, then at least it reduced the immediate tensions, and Jake saw that he was not alone in his new family situation.

I must note that I also found it hard to adjust to our new arrangement and to my life with both Jake and Sara. On one hand, I tried to pretend that we could form one happy family and that Sara had merely replaced Rachel as Jake's mother. On the other, I jealously guarded my own relationship with Jake and would constantly mediate between him and Sara, acting as a go-between in their arguments and in most of their other interactions. My ambivalence, I later found, stemmed from my inability to accept completely the ending of my first marriage and from my desire to hang on to its memory by excluding Sara from full participation with Jacob. Allowing her to really stand alone with him would have meant that the marriage with Rachel was finally over and that I irrevocably had to face new decisions in my life. Sara, for her part, had her own divided feelings about mothering this child which was not her own, while at the same time she harbored resentments about my attempts to exclude her from his relationship with me. And so the three of us engaged in a long and complex struggle, one which extended over years. Although this conflict gradually abated with the passage of time, it still flares up even today. Sara is not Jacob's mother, and he is not her son. I sometimes find myself caught between these two people that I love, and I face the need to devise ways to act as Jacob's parent while still encouraging Sara and Jake to forge their own relationship. The fairy tales had it right, I think, in portraying the difficulties of stepparents and stepchildren.

In the first weeks after Sara moved into my apartment, I became relatively unavailable to her. The fact that she moved to my place and renounced her previous living arrangements meant that she found herself in rather alien territory. Even though my apartment was more comfortable and convenient than hers, she sometimes felt that the move violated her feminist beliefs and that it constituted a return to the days when women automatically moved for their men. I reacted against her expression of such doubts (possibly from a sense that they were actually well-founded), and, at the same time, I experienced a sense of dread at the prospect of sharing my life with Sara on a more permanent basis.

The move took place in midsummer, and I managed to find time to run many miles in the long evenings and then to put away a couple of gin and tonics or a few beers. When Sara returned each night from work I would be sufficiently exhausted or potted or withdrawn to avoid making real contact with her. I secretly nursed my frustration at her seeming encroachment on my time and space, and at her own mixed feelings about this move; I also experienced regret that my days as an independent man had come to an end. Finally, Sara complained of my unavailability, and I countered with my objections to what I took as a drain on my independence and energy. After much discussion, we both came to realize that such struggles were part of the normal process of taking another step toward each other. We each harbored divided feelings about this process and about the mutual vulnerability that increased intimacy might entail. With the aid of our therapists, we eventually came to realize that although such trepidations were well-founded, we could confront them together and that we were not condemned merely to reproduce failed relationships of the past. We could continue as a couple by making our divided feelings as clear to each other as possible.

Beginning a relationship is difficult. Helping it to grow is perhaps harder. Although our discussions and disclosures were important, at various moments I found myself resisting the deliberate effort to build our commitment. I told myself that things were better when men and women just joined together for better or worse. Enough of this constant analysis of our feelings and of the process of forming a relationship! Perhaps in the end our efforts could be no more a guide to success than Woody Allen's dictum in *Annie Hall*: "Relationships are like sharks; they have to move forward or die." Well, we had moved forward together. Our love was seemingly nourished by the daily disclosure of feelings—our affections as well as our resentments and hopes. But this process often gave signs of devouring all our time and energy, leaving very little for anything but the effort to understand and to come close to each other. Yet, I had to admit that the means we had chosen to help solidify our love had aided us in traversing the initial rocky places. If we were to stay together, then I had to assume that Sara and I would continue to make the time to disclose our feelings. This was a process which I came to learn as an adult, and which, I guess, constitutes a sign of my own growing maturity. I do not believe, however, that it provides an ideal path to commitment for everyone. What helps one couple might not help another.

I found, in addition, that I had learned from the mistakes and lessons of my former marriage. Although in our time together Sara and I have worked to achieve a certain equality, it is an equality based less on a precisely apportioned division of labor (as was the case with Rachel and me) than upon an awareness of our individual needs. The success of a relationship today may often require an equitable division of the mundane tasks of life. As are many of the men interviewed for this book, I am concerned with doing my part to maintain the house and to perform necessary chores. In addition to such traditionally "masculine" tasks as carrying out the trash and keeping up with essential repairs, I do the weekly laundry, help in preparing the meals and washing dishes, and I usually vacuum the floors. Sara, for her part, does most of the weekly shopping, makes many of the dinners, folds and puts away the wash, and does most of the lawn and garden maintenance. We both pay the bills and keep a running account of our household expenses, maintaining for that purpose a joint bank account which often has its funds raided to pay for various personal expenses. Our division of labor is rather rough, and we tend to work out the separation of responsibilities less by careful negotiation than by following our own personal preferences.

Somehow, together we manage to accomplish the jobs at hand, and though at times we still struggle over who is responsible for a number of daily tasks, we so far have been able to do this with only a modicum of friction. If Sara feels that she sometimes would like me to make more dinners, I might also like her to be more responsible for keeping the house clean and for not expecting me always to do the traditional "masculine" duties of household repair. Such a list of chores might seem rather petty, but the chores must get done, no matter who is responsible for them. I am convinced, however, that a long-term relationship—even the most romantic relationship—often must involve a successful repetition of these mundane tasks. If one or the other partner feels badly used in the course of the daily rounds or feels oppressed by a too precise and burdensome division of labor, it can ultimately threaten the relationship. We all must live from day to day as well as in the peak moments of our time together, and in the words of Boston Gestalt psychologist Michael V. Miller, the daily round of our lives presents innumerable opportunities for the partners in a relationship to terrorize, threaten, and undermine each other.[3] I think that the key to maintaining a healthy link between the daily tasks of life and the underlying bedrock of love is the ability to negotiate without feeling oppressed: the ability, in other words, to talk about the things one must get done in order for both people to be able to function, and about what contributes reasonable expectations. This might preclude what might be considered precise and equal division of labor, but over time and with a good deal of open and direct discussion, a rough equality can be maintained. The essential element (in this and in so much else in a relationship or a marriage) is that both partners express their feelings and needs without fear of being overwhelmed or psychologically assaulted by the other.

As we have seen, numerous contemporary men feel especially pressured by demands imposed by child care, particularly after long days at work outside the home. This was one of the shoals on which my marriage to Rachel foundered, for neither of us was prepared for the daily, insistent demands of caring for a young child. For most men—raised mainly by mothers as we were—knowing how to deal with a child is not an "automatic" part of our repertoire. Moreover, there still remains a resistance to doing what we've been taught to consider essentially "women's work." Although obviously there can be great gratification in caring for one's own child, for many adult males there persists a gnawing sense that we have more important things to accomplish than to be stuck changing diapers, feeding a drooling infant, or arranging for playmates or babysitters. According to one of the truest descriptions I ever heard, child care tends "to turn the adult mind to mush." Since contemporary middle-class men work mainly with their minds, we can ill afford to allow our minds to become mushy—or so we feel. We also often think that we are "too good" to play an equal role in the care of children or in domestic chores, and that if we must take part (and today, many of us do take some part) we should, in the words of one of the men whom I interviewed, "let the women direct the traffic," and provide a child care schedule for us. When I again father a son or daughter, I know that Sara and I will need to find an equitable way to resolve the dilemma of child care. I cannot expect her to give up her own professional career to stay at home with an infant, and I cannot afford to do the same. Neither can I rely on her to "direct the traffic" while I mostly stand around waiting for orders.

In the absence of adequate day-care facilities in the United States and, even more, in the absence of male responsibility for sharing all aspects of child rearing, the issue of who will raise the children must continue to haunt us. We must deal with the question of who will sacrifice what part of self and of career to care for children, and ultimately the question of what effect it has on a child to be brought up mainly by mother or father or by some fairly equal combination of the two.[4]

The provision of emotional support and understanding is crucial in the relationship of men and women, a foundation on which all else must rest. In the years we have been together, Sara and I have usually been able to give that support. I cannot say how we found that we could do this, but when she comes home from a strenuous day at work, or when I have had a hard time with my writing, or at the times when I might miss Jake, now mainly living with Rachel far away, Sara and I can usually stop what we are doing and contend with our feelings. At such moments, we might sit down to a long, slow, candle-lit dinner and review the day's events in minute detail. In fact, one of the hidden benefits from a recent spell of unemployment (a period which in other ways was very painful), was that I was able to learn how to cook and to prepare those dinners with a thoughtful selection of wine and with flowers on the table. The preparation of fine foods—French sauces or extravagant desserts—always seemed one more bit of alien female territory, but here I was, working in the kitchen, juggling three or four courses, thinking about my presentation of each dish, and anticipating Sara's arrival from the daily wars with the expectation that we would then sit down, have a drink, and begin to clear away the stress of the day. At first, I felt wary of this seeming reversal of roles. Then it became clear that our relationship had grown and benefited from my time of enforced idleness, that we could now take care of each other in new and surprising ways. I became not only *maitre d'* and chef, but counselor and confessor, offering Sara solace for the slings and arrows, dealing with her work issues, taking vicarious pleasure in her daily triumphs and feeling regret for her losses while also attempting to resolve whatever arguments she and I might have together. I had, without premeditation, begun to explore what might be called the feminine side of myself, but which perhaps is better called the more affective side, since both men and women are capable of affection and affectivity.

This period ended and I returned to full-time work. I was elated that I was again doing a man's job. I was now contributing a fair portion of our earnings, and I felt good about myself in a rather traditional masculine way. Within a short time, however, I realized that I missed taking primary responsibility for the house, for orchestrating those meals and for establishing the context of our time together. Sara and I still share those warm moments when we can confront our cares and dilemmas and our mutual disputes and when we can have a nice dinner and a glass of wine, but such moments now seem more rushed and less carefully prepared. We still try to deal fairly and honestly with our feelings for and against each other, but we must work harder to create a setting in which we can safely ventilate our emotions. I feel a sense of loss at now having less time to respond to Sara's daily needs and to be responsible for emotional support, for cooking enticing meals, and for home making.

After a long period of hesitation and discussion, Sara and I eventually decided to get married. This was not an easy decision. Our discussion of it took place over many months and at the cost of much anxiety for both of us. Although I wanted to marry Sara, I feared the consequences of this step, for a new marriage might be reminiscent of my earlier one. Sara, for her part, threatened to leave me if I could not make a further commitment (how serious was this threat, I'll never know), and she virtually asked me to propose formally to her.

Although Sara and I experienced much turmoil over our decision to marry, Jacob's anxiety once again surpassed ours, for he worried (as he said) that if Sara and I married, he would be forced to give us his love for his mother. As he put it, "My father's wife then automatically becomes my mother, right?" Although we attempted to convince him that Rachel would always be his mother, and that Sara would remain as a stepparent, he continued to make it clear that he felt very insecure about our plans. When all three of us went to pick out napkins and tablecloths for our wedding reception, Jacob threw a tantrum in the store and refused to speak to us. He remained disconsolate right up to the day of the wedding, and it was only after much negotiation that he agreed to take part in the ceremony.

I must admit, however, that my own behavior was not much better than Jacob's. Because of my uncertainty, I had trouble remembering whom we had invited to the wedding and details of our plans. I finally refused pointblank to concern myself with any further preparations (figuratively stamping my feet in a manner reminiscent of my son's tantrum). I felt deeply divided and ambivalent about the decision to turn a cohabitative relationship into a marriage, and out of my own confusion and defensiveness I even denied to Sara that I experienced any ambivalent feeling.

Finally, I came to accept the fact that if I wanted to continue my relationship with Sara, the time had come to put it on a still more regular and intentional basis, and I sat down to talk with her about what we might be able to pledge to each other in our marriage. We both agreed that we did not want merely to promise, "for richer or poorer, in sickness or in health . . ." in the traditional manner, but that we wanted to embody in words the essence of the process of commitment and negotiation that had been central to the development of our love. We both decided that we would simply vow to express ourselves as openly as possible and to be as honest as we could. These are perhaps not very profound sentiments, but they are vital, nonetheless. Our wedding, far from being a family-run affair, was put on entirely by our friends. They provided the food and drink and even the place where the wedding was held. The wedding celebrated not only our commitment to each other, but it shared that commitment with the community of friends and colleagues of which we felt ourselves a part. Rather than a ritual paean to preordained ideas of marriage and family, the ceremony was a way for Sara and I to reaffirm our love.

I think that with Sara I have finally come to understand some fundamentals about love relationships, and I have found ways to resolve a few of the dilemmas of contemporary masculinity. Men *can* break down some of the rigid sex role behavior which formerly served to define and limit us. We no longer need to fulfill only certain prescribed functions, but we can now do much that previously was forbidden. We can express feelings, we can take care of the house and children, we can cook or bake, we can show sadness and be emotionally supportive of our mates. In addition, I have learned that love relationships are creatures of evolution and change. They are built not so much on hope for an idealized future as upon the ability to deal with the survival needs of the present as well as the daily permutation of our emotions. A partner is not a parent: she is a lover, a friend, a helper, and a counselor, but I cannot expect her to be there always to take care of my needs. I've come to realize, as well, that our time here is too short to sweat the small stuff—so arguments should be clean, and one should be prepared to surrender the most impregnable positions for the good of the relationship.

In his recent book, *The Masculine Dilemma*, Dr. Gregory Rochlin argues that men can never hope to resolve in adult life the essential turmoil of childhood and youth. "The dilemmas that are endemic to the masculine experience are played out again and again," Rochlin contends. "The purchase of masculinity is never fully secured." According to Rochlin, our male self-esteem is precariously based, whether early in life or late, and we are besieged by a "unique vulnerability to failed expectations," a vulnerability which promotes the outsized masculine ego, as well as male defensiveness and male aggression.[5] Perhaps this is true in some ultimate sense. I know, however, that in my own life I have been able to find some pathways to growth through the hard lessons of an ended marriage and a new commitment. Such new commitment is with a woman who wants to be with a man on the basis of equality, and who respects me for not pretending to superiority and for not attempting to take care of her in a traditional fashion. We might both still be uneasy about the new expectations which confront men and women today, but we have found some ways to overcome our ambivalent and divided feelings.

Specifically, I have learned, first, that one can insure some degree of continuity in relationships by being willing to negotiate about everything.

Second, I have learned to hide neither appreciation nor resentment, but to give voice to as many of my feelings as possible and to listen to those of my partner with as little defensiveness as I can muster.

Third, I have found that I must continue to negotiate, discuss, and listen every day of my life with Sara, and that I must be available to share and divide the mundane and indispensable tasks of daily living. I have learned not to avoid confrontations in the name of an idealized perfection, but to enter into such struggles in the hope that they will produce resolution and change. As Sara told me, "We've fought every inch of the way, and I guess that we'll fight as long as we're together." Fighting need not be fatal as long as one can end each argument cleanly and can get beneath the surface to discover the ultimate and hidden sources of disagreement.

Finally, I have learned that when the above resolutions fail to bring relief and when two people can no longer move forward together, then it is worthwhile to get some professional therapeutic help and not to be reluctant to admit this need.

Perhaps the steps I have just outlined will not guarantee instant success in a love relationship, but they have made sense for Sara and me. Adopting such a strategy has helped me understand that—in contrast to Dr. Rochlin's pessimistic assessment—one can change and grow without much worry about ultimate failure or about the collapse of one's expectations. Sara and I might fail in our life together, or we might continue together. The main question is not the final result, but the quality of daily experience. I consider myself to have attained a more solid manhood, and I have come to realize that beginning again with someone new can offer the prospect for growth. I think that I am now with a person whom I can trust and who can trust me, and that we meet each other as mature individuals. The road here was hard. It is nice to have gotten this far.

Notes

1. See Robert Weiss, *Marital Separation* (New York: Basic Books, 1975), Chapters 4–5.
2. Bernie Zilbergeld, *Male Sexuality* (New York: Bantam, 1978), p. 4.
3. Michael V. Miller, in conversation. See Michael V. Miller, "Intimate Terrorism," in *Psychology Today*, April, 1977.
4. See James A. Levine, *Who Will Raise the Children? New Options for Fathers (and Mothers)* (Philadelphia and New York: J. B. Lippincott, 1976); David B. Lynn, *The Father: His Role in Child Development* (Monterey, California: Brooks/Cole, 1974); Dorothy Dinnerstein, *The Mermaid and the Minotaur* (New York: Harper, 1976); Nancy Chodorow, *The Reproduction of Mothering* (Berkeley and Los Angeles: University of California Press, 1978).
5. Gregory Rochlin, *The Masculine Dilemma* (Boston: Little, Brown and Co., 1980), pp. x–xl.

CHAPTER 6

Men Working

[Work], by its very nature, [is] about violence—to the spirit as well as to the body. It is about ulcers as well as accidents, about shouting matches as well as fistfights, about nervous breakdowns as well as kicking the dog around. It is, above all (or beneath all) about daily humiliations. To survive the day is triumph enough for the walking wounded among the great many of us.

—STUDS TERKEL, *Working*

Work is dignity, and the only dignity.

—F. SCOTT FITZGERALD, *The Letters of F. Scott Fitzgerald*

Work has always been a central concern in the lives of men. Traditionally, in Western society a man's sense of himself was derived mainly from his daily labor. To be a man meant to practice one's trade and to take one's place in a community of labor—a community which provided not only a livelihood, but a role in the world, and often even a family name: Miller, Baker, Carter, Smith, Thatcher. Work still retains a vital place in our lives, and many recent commentators on male experience see the resolution of work-based issues as critical in traversing successfully the various stages of masculine development. Daniel Levinson (1978) speaks of "seasons of a man's life" which are largely oriented around problems of career and work. Gail Sheehy (1976) similarly speaks of life-passages which for men revolve around crises and transitions in work; while for Gregory Rochlin work is a basis for the "manly deeds" and worldly achievements that indicate the growth of adult control. Erik Erikson, perhaps the most respected authority on life-cycle development, sees adulthood as a time concerned with issues of generativity—that is, with production and creativeness in relation as much to the material world as to one's own family.[1]

I must confess my misgivings about placing this chapter on work so late in the discussion. If work is basic to male development and experience, such a chapter should presumably stand somewhere near the beginning of this exploration. Why, then, should a discussion of work appear near the end? The answer, I think, is fairly simple, and it serves to mark the distance between contemporary male experience and the views of even some of the most recent commentators on the male life-cycle. Writers such as Levinson and Sheehy—while accurate in many respects—have focused their attention primarily on a more traditional world in which issues of male work tended to come first and in which questions concerning relationships and marriage, while important, were often secondary. Women served largely in a supportive capacity—keeping the home fires burning, caring for children and the domestic nest, encouraging men in their careers. If issues of divorce and starting new relationships arose, they often did so in connection with a so-called "mid-life crisis," a time when men suddenly began to reevaluate their past lives and to question settled marriages and jobs.[2]

I believe that in contrast to these findings, many men in today's world continually re-examine their lives—during their twenties and thirties as well as in the mid-life decades. Basic to this constant probing (at least in my own experience and in that of men whom I have interviewed) is a sense that relationships and personal issues must often take precedence over work. It is possible, of course, to work hard at a career at any time—in one's twenties as well as afterward—but it seems that many of us feel that we cannot devote full energy to a career path until issues of love are resolved. As I found in my own life, it was necessary to establish a trusting relationship before I could move on to questions of maturity and accomplishment in work.

It is not easy, however, to make clear distinctions between issues of love and work when we confront them on a daily basis. Much of the tension that we feel in arriving at a firm self-definition arises from the conflict between the traditional pull of work and the insistent demands which emerge from our changing personal relationships. In addition to an income, work can provide status, growth, a sense of accomplishment, and meaning. Trying to satisfy all these needs through our daily labor tends to make work a source of considerable anxiety. Additional pressures to change our work lives in relation to women has served to increase the tension. For example, Stan notes in speaking of these issues:

> It's now critical for me to find some balance between my commitment to my career and my relationship with Amy, a balance which seems often

to shift. Sometimes, my workload gets heavier and this gives me less free time at home or less energy to build our life together. At other times, I limit my career effort to be with Amy, but this also means that I have to give up income which is important to maintaining our style of life. So there is a constant trade for me between various options and demands.

I've begun to think, however, that having a certain job or profession is secondary to who I am as a person. It is really difficult to find a worthwhile love relationship, and I often think that maybe I should put more into my relationship than into work. I don't think that love must necessarily come before career, but I always find myself attempting to weigh one against the other and to take care of things in both spheres.

I think that I've become more willing to do things that will help my relationship to grow, and it's probable that many men now feel this way. Previously, it was understood that the man would go out and make the bucks, and that the woman would stay home with the kids. The fact that women have recently gone out to work has had a major impact. In a way, you must now share her with the world. Ironically, this has served to make our relationship even more important. It becomes more valuable to be together in the time available and to gain strength from each other.

Andy Brown, an attorney in his mid-thirties, similarly told me about his new attitude toward work. "My divorce was crucial in helping to re-evaluate my priorities in relation to career and family. When I was just out of law school, I placed a lot of expectations on myself which I had accepted from who knows where. Initially, my work took precedence. But as I got into my profession, accompanied by an increasing amount of dissatisfaction in my first marriage, I began to realize that my career success, while important, was not as crucial as I first thought. Now, when I look at career, it is something that is meaningful and important as a life's activity, but I think that the predominant feature of my life is my relationship with Karen—my second wife—and with my family. The career is meaningful and something that I enjoy doing and that I need for my own personal development, but in some ways it's almost secondary to the relationship. If something were to happen and I couldn't continue in my career, this probably would not be as difficult as not continuing the relationship. I seem now to have a very different set of priorities than in my first marriage."

If development of a new sense of relationship often takes precedence in the lives of contemporary men, the issues of work and career still remain important. Curiously, I found out the most about work and its bearing upon my own sense of maleness by not having any formal work during my several months of unemployment. I also discovered how my growing ability to share in a love relationship helped to resolve the doubts and fears imposed by this time of enforced and discomforting idleness. Since my teen-age years I had worked more or less steadily at a variety of jobs: first at part-time jobs of the sort that one found in high school and college—busboy, waiter, life guard, dish washer, delivery truck driver—and then at more "serious" full-time employment as a budding professional and academic. In youth (and mostly during summers) I had sampled the meaning and nature of the 9-to-5 grind, whether delivering telephone books in the central city, driving a truck for a furniture warehouse, or washing dishes in the depths of a restaurant kitchen. What I learned from that experience was a profound sense of how hard most people must labor to make ends meet, how life-draining is the daily thralldom to bosses and foremen, and how—to borrow Studs Terkel's words—work in this society could often be described as violence to the flesh as well as humiliation to the soul. Partly to escape such a fate I became an academic and a teacher—work which seemed relatively free from the normal quotient of pain and drudgery and which appeared to allow the preservation of dignity and ideals.

Suddenly, I was without work. The academic employment crunch of the 1970's had swept away my teaching job as it had that of so many others, and I found myself one summer day standing at the end of a long, slow line in my local unemployment office. As I waited in that thoroughly democratic line along with house painters and construction men, secretaries, mechanics, and occasional white-collar employees, I contemplated the painful loss of prestige and esteem which such a wait seemed to mean. Not only was I temporarily without funds and forced into dependence on the largesse of the Employment Security Office, but I felt denied a hard-earned place on a career ladder and the status that a climb on that ladder seemed to bring.

There is another side to this story, which has to do with the salutary loss of a sense of "entitlement" and privilege. A wait in the unemployment line quickly removes a sense of qualification and priority and while this is an uncomfortable lesson to learn, it has an importance of its own. In contemporary society (as Richard Sennett and Jonathan Cobb have pointed out in *The Hidden Injuries of Class*)[3] manual work is systematically depreciated and brain work exalted: a situation which serves to undermine the self-esteem of those who must earn their daily bread by the work of their hands. In the unemployment line one quickly discovers that all are equal and that all are struggling with the pain and humiliation of becoming an unwanted cog in the economic machine.

Finally, it was my turn to present my social security card and to tell my story to the clerk who waited behind the desk.

"Your previous job?"

"College Professor."

"Uhuh. Just sign this form and please sit over there until your name is called."

I waited on a bench perhaps a half-hour more, and finally I was shown into an ante-room with about a dozen other applicants to hear a lecture on the nature of unemployment insurance and our responsibilities to the system.

"You have an obligation to your former employer," a bureaucrat of middle years told us. "They are paying for your time on unemployment, and so we want to get you off the rolls as quickly as possible. We are going to ask you to have interviews with three prospective employers a week, and you might not be able to find the same kind of work as before. We'll be checking on you, so no loafing and no excuses." Silently I tried to appreciate the irony of this moment, and I wondered if the lecturer to whom I listened with such trepidation could ever have been interested in attending the lectures that I prided myself on having given, lectures which I worked hard to prepare and which I considered competent performances in my trade. And almost despite myself—and my initial anger—I began to feel sorry for this public functionary. I wondered how often he had to deliver the same diatribe—twice a week? five times? ten times? He was condemned to this office while at least I could leave when his homily had finished. It seemed that everyone became diminished in this situation.

Unemployment was instructive in other ways. It was a time, as I have said, when Sara and I experienced a sharp reversal of our usual roles. Although I looked forward to taking care of the house for a while and to preparing meals, I never imagined what would happen when Sara actually became the principal wage earner. Some nights she would arrive angry and upset, and I would then retaliate in kind. When we were finally able to discuss our disagreements, she told me of her fear that I would never find another full-time job and that I would remain dependent on her forever. Even though she was a professional woman and had systematically given up many inherited women's ideas about work and its meaning, one deeply ingrained bit of training remained:

the feeling that women should not support men, even if the time of such necessity might actually be short. These questions created a dreadful sense of lost boundaries—perhaps my unemployment wouldn't be so temporary? Perhaps she had taken on a role for which she was not prepared? It was difficult for her to earn the money while I remained home to do the dishes, shop, and cook dinner.

I had to confess to similar fears. A man was supposed to be *the* breadwinner or at least (in my newly amended sex-role consciousness) *a* breadwinner. To be less was less than a man. How long could my self-esteem survive this reversal? How long could our new marriage survive? Sharing these doubts made things easier for both of us. I came to be able to make some of my inner turmoil accessible. Sara was able to share her fears about the expectation that she should do more than her required share as a woman. In understanding our ambivalence about the change from earlier models of male and female behavior, and in learning how deeply ingrained were those earlier models, we came, I think, to love each other all the more and finally to strengthen our marriage.

Many men seem confused by changing work roles. Psychologist Sam Doucet, for example, notes that when he married a few years ago, his wife Paula was working, and he was between clinical jobs: "I had no money and she was supporting both of us, and I really understood how a housewife must feel about being stuck at home. I also felt like I was a fugitive from justice and that the police might soon pick me up for vagrancy. I would spend all day fantasizing about Paula coming home and seeing all the things I had done around the house, but in reality I never felt that I got enough praise. She was at work, and she really didn't have time to appreciate what I was doing. Generally, I liked the time off that I had, but it also was very uncomfortable for me. I had a lot of divided feelings about being taken care of by her, and I think that I sometimes slipped into the idea that I was a little boy and she was a mother—especially during times of a money crunch. When money issues came up I would feel dependent in this new situation."

Now, the circumstances are almost exactly reversed. Paula is expecting a baby, and Sam must prepare to be the sole breadwinner for a time.

> When Paula recently quit her job near the end of her pregnancy the change really got to me. I became worried that certain understandings

in our relationship were to be broken. Ever since I went back to full-time work I have liked our arrangement of dividing things evenly: that Paula takes care of herself, and I take care of myself, and that we meet together. When she stays home now she's much more involved in domestic chores. She's gotten into doing things that I usually take care of, like fixing up the house (but maybe that's her need to create a nest for the baby) and I have come to feel that something is being taken away from me in terms of what I really like to do.

I now have to carry most of the financial burden, as well, and although Paula took on this responsibility when I was out of work, I haven't felt particularly good about having it all on my shoulders. When this first happened, I began to feel that we were actually going backwards to a traditional male-female division of labor. I began to see myself as the lonely worker, working my ass off in a rather traditional setting. I had always said that I wanted to have kids, but when it really happened I became immediately angry that she was going to have a nice thing with the baby and that I was going to have to go off and work fifty or sixty hours a week to support both of them. I began to see myself as no longer part of the family but as the work horse who was somehow to be forgotten.

The way we began to deal with this was in the setting of a professional group with whom we met every few weeks. This group is not engaged strictly in mutual support or therapy, but it mostly discusses work-related problems. We were both finally able to speak our minds about our changing work roles in the setting of the group, and a lot of our mutual tension and anxiety began to come out. That, in turn, set off a discussion between us that lasted for several days about how she was feeling, about leaving work, and about the kinds of burdens I was feeling. Somehow we started to communicate more openly.

The problem is that before this we hadn't really talked about our changing roles and what they were going to be. We had struggled to bring about an equally shared relationship and suddenly we found ourselves regressing to a more traditional place, and we both felt a lot of worry and resentment about this.

Eventually, I would like to return to some sort of equality of sharing both inside and outside the house when the child is about six months old. I have protective feelings for Paula, and our current arrangement is now more comfortable for me, but it might be really different if Paula said she didn't want to go back to work at all. Even with a kid I can see her working a reduced schedule. I feel that I can manage for six months or a year. But I don't like being the sole family support indefinitely. I really get no satisfaction from taking care of someone financially, and I would feel very resentful if that happened indefinitely.

Other issues about changing work requirements have arisen for Edwin Bard, a business entrepreneur in his mid-thirties. A few years ago Edwin relinquished a successful career in advertising to open a chain of stores which he manages with Ellen, the woman with whom he lives. This was a difficult decision because it meant renouncing his conventional ideas of career success in exchange for the chance of integrating his work and his love relationship.

For me the hard thing is not learning to adjust to a "new role as a male," that is, to everyday questions about who does the vacuuming or cleaning, or to new sexual mores or attitudes. The problem is adjusting to a different *image* of what a man is—adjusting to a different idea of success, of a job, a career, and then finding ways to like myself. When I achieved success in my former career, I liked myself fine, but I wasn't happy. And now what I'm trying to do is to like myself, but to have a different vision of success. Learning to adjust, but also to like myself is the question.

With the shift in my circumstances, it's hard to get a notion of one's true male self. That version of "true self" is so ephemeral that one day I can think that I'm on the right track in balancing work against a good and happy home life, and the next day I'll be dissatisfied, and I'll think that I'm not achieving what I should in light of my experience and my aspirations. A main task now is to try to figure out how to get a real balance between family, relationship, and career, and this is probably the key issue for many men like me.

Even though my corporate job provided security and status, it was boring. I found myself waiting for secretaries to bring xeroxes around or for guys to get out of meetings, and on the day that I finally decided to quit, I actually caught myself making faces into the glass covering a framed graphic on my wall. Boredom had a lot to do with my decision to leave. Even though I was called upon to handle some big accounts, I didn't think that what I did was that important. Even more, my decision to leave that job was based on my relationship with Ellen. The decision came at a pivotal point, and had I decided to stay in New York, the relationship would have fallen apart. She was happy in this town, as I was, when I visited her here; so I decided to move to be with her. It was a point when something had to give. My job was taking a high toll on me personally, and I didn't want it to destroy my relationship, as well. I wondered which was more important: the rewards of my relationship with this woman, or a job that I wasn't even crazy about?

Coming to accept relationships in which both partners maintain a career has been rewarding but difficult for many men. It is now estimated that only about one-fourth of American families live in the traditional setting of the male-headed household in which the father provides the sole income for wife and children. Changing social customs, the women's movement, and the depredations of inflation have all combined to render the conventional family pattern almost as obsolete as the high-powered gas-guzzling automobile.

In my own life I have become increasingly familiar with the problems of juggling two careers. In my first marriage, Rachel struggled to free herself from traditional expectations that she be wife and mother and little else. She strove tenaciously to find work which would somehow flow from her new concern with feminine questions. At first, she organized discussion groups for women on a professional basis. Eventually, she joined with several other women to produce a number of valuable studies of feminist issues and was thus able to launch an increasingly successful career.

My response to these developments was inconsistent. I felt on one hand a sense of admiration for Rachel's ingenuity and her commitment to make a career from her vital personal concerns. I hoped also that her career could add substantially to our family income and could help ease what seemed to me the burden of the sole wage earner. Ideally, I thought, we would both benefit from her growing success, and that this would eventually help strengthen our relationship. We would increasingly share income, house care, child care, and our emotional life. We would, in effect, be pioneers in largely uncharted territory.

On the other hand, I felt outraged and betrayed by Rachel's new career interest. This was not part of what I had assumed our marriage would be. I was secretly angry that Rachel would no longer depend on me as the family breadwinner, while in a contradictory way, I was also upset that she did not earn as much as she had promised. I was annoyed that she still seemed to want my emotional support, and I was fearful at the same time that her career would eventually outstrip my own. While I consciously suppressed such feelings, not wishing to appear vulnerable or unsupportive, I withdrew icily or I picked arguments over trivial matters. Rachel, for her part, fought me to a standstill. Whether the issue was how much time was available for each of us to work, or who would do child care or wash the dishes, a good part of our life was spent in recrimination and hostility.

It is difficult now to unravel the contradictory and often irrational roots of our disagreements. I have come to recognize, however, that such ambiguous feelings are common to families in the throes of change. My conversations with other men have helped me understand that many of us share similar fears and anxieties. Learning to deal with such fears is a task that we all confront in the changing world of work and personal life. We could, of course, choose to ignore such concerns, or we could accept the dictums of George Gilder and other anti-feminist publicists and thus actively resist the alterations in our lives.[4] I am convinced, however, that a hostile reaction will do little to affect the underlying sources of current change. Like it or not, the world has altered dramatically and the best course is to respond in a positive and supportive manner. Women are pursuing their own careers, and they will continue to do so. It is now up to men to adjust as gracefully as possible and to learn to share both professional opportunities and daily household duties. In the words of the Chinese fortune cookie: "The best way to deal with change is to become part of it."

My relationship with Sara has helped me alter my former course. As I have said, she is a woman who knew from the very beginning that she wanted a serious and successful career, and thus we came together knowing that this would always be part of our life. I have learned to make my concern about the loss of traditional prerogatives more clear, and to discuss my anxieties with her. I am still sometimes afraid that I might take second place to her career needs, or that her ability to support herself will eventually enable her to move out of our marriage. I have found that merely giving voice to my fears helps to dispel their threat. Confession does seem to be good for the soul, even when it is a confession of fears rather than of sins. Unnamed and scarcely conscious forebodings can be reduced by bringing them into the light of day. Surprisingly, it appears that making oneself vulnerable in this manner serves not to weaken but to strengthen a relationship.

Some concrete problems remain, however. I recently commuted to a job over a long distance, and I needed to be away from home several nights a week. Many dual-career families maintain such a pattern. In one extreme case with which I am familiar, the husband works in Montreal while the wife works in Denver, and each of them travels to the other's city on alternate weekends. Such an arrangement (albeit in a less extreme form) proved impossible for Sara and me. We came to realize that our marriage is based solidly on a commitment to be with each other daily. When we are not together for a night or two we feel that much time has passed and that we are out of phase with the major events in each other's life. Eventually, it became necessary to consolidate our circumstances, and only through much discussion and with much misgiving could we resolve to move to the location of my employment. My job, we both concluded, was the less mobile of the two, and Sara could more readily find employment where I worked than vice versa. Still, this decision was difficult for both of us. Sara felt resentful that after all the talk of equality, a woman seemed forced to move for a man when the chips were down. I felt guilty that I had torn her from a fruitful career and from supportive colleagues. I also experienced a sense of defensiveness in that I might again be perceived as a hypocrite, my actions belying my words.

Such issues are difficult for dual-career couples, and they occur with some regularity. They tend to raise questions about which partner has the most important career and the most power in a relationship.[5] They also promote the kinds of confrontations in which no one wins and everyone loses. If a couple finally relocates for a man's job, then the woman often feels resentful; if the move is for her job, the man may feel his competence is challenged. It required several months for Sara and me to understand the issues at stake in our impending move and for us to diffuse the resentment and guilt which the move entailed. I cannnot report that we completely quelled these feelings of anger and remorse; they still remain and sometimes surface in our daily lives.

Other issues revolve around how income is to be divided and bills to be paid. In contrast with more traditional work patterns, both partners earn their share and both must apportion a percentage for mutual needs and for their own individual purposes. As I have mentioned, Sara and I both maintain individual bank accounts and also a joint account which we employ for collective expenses. This plan seems to operate well, but at times neither of us takes as much responsibility for the joint budget as for our own personal accounts. We do not have a clear division for sharing expenses, but we attempt to consult each other about purchases and who should make them. We also attempt to alternate monthly in the balancing of the "household" account and paying monthly bills. For us, this plan works better than if all shared expenses were taken care of by one or the other partner.

There are many dual-career couples who follow such a pattern. Andy Brown, for example, notes that his wife takes care of paying all their bills, although they both pay equally into a joint checking account. "Mainly," Andy says, "this is because Karen is better at keeping accounts than I am and so she does it herself, paying our bills, and balancing the checkbook. We plan together for the household expenses but she actually pays them. She's very concerned with knowing how much money is available and where it is going."

Still another issue pertains to housework in a dual-career relationship—how the cooking and cleaning gets apportioned in a household in which both partners pursue outside careers. In the case of Sara and myself we seem to allot housework mainly on the basis of what needs to be accomplished and who is immediately available to accomplish it. When I'm home during the day, I'll prepare dinner, or I'll take major responsibility for the laundry. Sara will make dinners when she is able, or we'll both pitch in together to cook and to clean up. Such an informal relationship seems, in fact, to work better than those which are more formally contrived. Rachel and I, for example, attempted to apportion all household chores evenly, and this gave rise to bitterness when one of us did not accomplish the assigned task. We had little flexibility in such a pattern and not much room to negotiate. The main thing, I think, is to have insight into how such household tasks might also represent larger issues in the relationship. As one man told me, "Sometimes, my wife might come home late from work for a week or so, and I'll get angry about having to start dinners for all those nights. Partly, I'm upset at doing the extra work, but partly also what I'm saying is that I missed her for that time, and I wished that she'd come home earlier. These underlying feelings seem to get easily diverted for us into questions of work and responsibility around the house. On occasion the housework becomes a dumping ground for our other feelings."

Maintaining two careers provides certain advantages, however, and these are both material and psychological. Attorney Andy Brown notes, for example, that he and his wife could not imagine living any other way, and that their dual-career marriage has brought benefits to both of them. "One result of each having a full-time career is that we can afford a life-style that is somewhat comfortable in the face of inflation. One person doesn't have to bust their hump to be able to do it alone. A second advantage is that it brings a certain amount of health into the relationship. We both have something for ourselves and an identity outside the marriage, and to the extent that we both are doing something independently, it's refreshing to come back into the marriage together."

Andy relates that this has changed over time:

When Karen and I first started dating, we talked a lot about work, since we are both in the same professional field. That's no longer the case: we now spend very little time discussing the daily details of work. I think that our earlier need to talk over each aspect of work was a way to get to know each other, and that's no longer necessary. Karen and I have since learned to share lots of things not related to our work, so there is not much need to share all of our professional experiences. What generally does get discussed, however, are the major career frustrations, aggravations, and the hopes that we have. This has been nice, especially in comparison with the experience of my first marriage. Then, I didn't feel at all comfortable about coming home to talk about my frustrations and problems. Everything seemed to rest on my shoulders, for I was the sole breadwinner and my task was to keep my job and to be successful. It was too threatening to talk about the anxieties and fears of work. I felt that I had to be stable and to keep everything under control: this seemed a man's obligation and he couldn't share his feelings with his wife.

Now, it's nice to come home and to talk once in a while about my law practice and some of the problems and frustrations I encounter. Because Karen is an independent woman, she can be supportive without being overwhelmed by my feelings. The reverse is also true. I can do this for her, and she can share her happiness, fear, or sadness with me. In this way we are not just a "husband and wife" but two peers who talk together. Our relationship is not defined by some assigned sexual roles or by traditional rules, but more by mutual friendship.

Andy and Karen, however, are now planning to alter their division of labor. They are expecting a baby, and have been preparing to fit the experience of child-rearing into the existing structure of their lives. "I don't see too much of a problem in terms of how the new baby will affect our pattern of work," Andy says.

Right now, we're putting away half of Karen's income for the six months before the baby comes. She's planning to take a six month leave from her job, and we'll use these savings during this time. I'm restructuring my schedule so that I can be home some days, and when she goes back to work full-time, we'll continue to share child care, and we'll hire outside help for the time when we're not at home. Having a baby might cause some problems for us, but I don't think that they will be insurmountable. Having two careers has given us real flexibility. One of us can take off work for a time, and the other can then pick up the slack. Of course, I haven't spoken about how Karen might feel in losing six months from her career development. That's a real important issue for us both, and one we'll have to confront. But in general having two careers can help us more easily meet the changes in our lives.

Another dual-career pattern is exemplified by Edwin Bard, the ex-advertising executive who now runs a business with his mate. He and Ellen are partners both at home and at the office, and this arrangement might seem a breeding ground for a variety of problems. I feel that I'm sort of paving the way, Edwin says:

> I'm living in unexplored country, and I don't rely on the model of individual male success that was basic to my father or his generation of business men. Oddly enough, sharing the same business with Ellen seems in itself not such a big issue. We wanted to be together, and this might sound like pie-in-the-sky, but we feel now as if we can't be together enough. Sure, we have our differences over the business but they are no more significant than other differences that we might have. I definitely don't feel diminished by working closely with her, and it seems to me that a lot of men—even those who claim to be "liberated"—have a fear of being overshadowed by the capabilities of the women that they are with. Maybe I'm paying myself an unwarranted compliment, but I think that perhaps the ultimate liberation for men is not to feel threatened by the talents of women.
>
> I think that Ellen and I make a good team. She just happens to have a great aptitude for figures and for business calculations and dealings. She's good at handling the financial aspects of the business. If we have to go to our bank or our accountant, she's mastered the basics of our situation. I have other virtues, and she defers to me in those areas: promotion, sales, a lot of the buying and calculations in terms of volume, and this arrangement seems to work very well for us. There's always a potential for jealousy or resentment, I guess, but I have learned through my relationship with Ellen how to manage these feelings. Just because someone else is good at something, it doesn't mean that you are any less a person. So rather than a source of conflict, our work arrangement has helped us relieve a lot of pressure.

Edwin notes that he and Ellen work together at home in similar ways. "We have a division of labor both in business and in house care."

> We might need to vacuum the apartment and Ellen will say jokingly, 'that's a man's job,' and laundry will need to be done and I'll say, 'oh, that's a woman's job,' and we just divide things according to what needs to be accomplished and who feels better about doing it. I like to vacuum and she hates it. I hate to make the bed and she likes it. We sometimes have conflicts about such things and about work-related issues as well, but they are superseded by the knowledge that the tasks have to be done and so we try to negotiate about how to do them. I think that people of my generation—basically of the sixties and seventies—go into relationships knowing that questions and problems need to be worked out in all areas of our lives. Most of us who claim to be at all 'liberated' or enlightened assume that relationships will be like that.

Still another pattern is that adopted by Mike, whom we met in another chapter, and by Caroline, his wife. Each works only part-time outside the house, and they spend half their time taking care of domestic and child care needs. Mike feels that his ability to participate in this arrangement stems from his rather low-key attitude toward work success while he was growing up and from his resistance to traditional definition of male careers. "The sharing of house care and child care is a large priority for me," Mike notes:

> It would be a lot more difficult to split things evenly with Caroline if I were a man who was more career oriented. I've never been a person who was driven by career goals, and I never knew as a kid what I wanted to do when I got to be an adult. I always felt that I wanted to work with people, but that was about as specific as I got. In college I studied psychology, but since that turned out to be a study of rats more than of people, I became disaffected, and I ended up after college with no firm idea of what I wanted for a life's work. In the next few years I did a bunch of odd jobs, everything from fruit picking to house painting, and eventually, I became involved in teaching, first as a substitute teacher, and then on the regular payroll. You might say that I got into it in a very indirect manner: I was looking for a job, and work as a substitute teacher was available. I took it, and I'm still teaching, on a more or less part-time basis, but I didn't set out to do this in college and before.
>
> I'm happy, however, that I'm not working more hours outside the house. My profession and my work at home are complementary in many ways. As a teacher I can be somewhat extroverted, and I can get outside my own immediate concerns. Then I come home and take care of our son and daughter, and I'm kind of a househusband. I do much

of the cooking and cleaning, and the sort of energy required of me at work and at home seem to interact in very positive ways. Things have turned out very nicely, and I'm very happy with my career pursuits outside the house and my efforts at home. I think that as long as our children are young, Caroline and I will continue to split the time as we do, and afterwards I might go into a more full-time educational career, or I might do counseling with men and women on the problems they confront in life. I even might convert my hobby of building puppets into a career, but that is scary because it is even less traditional than what I'm now doing and because one really has to hustle to make it work. You might say, however, that I would like to continue to define my work in ways that are not very stereotyped and which don't involve a heavy trip about what masculine achievement might be about. Finally, my work life is built very basically on coordinating my pursuits and jobs with those of Caroline, as well.

A dual-career relationship cannot succeed for everyone. Nick Barnes is an architect who found that he and Liz, who plays flute professionally in a major orchestra, could not make the compromise necessary to combine their work and personal lives. "I felt pretty empty when we broke up over the issue of who would shift their work," Nick says:

Liz recently told me that at one time she would have changed jobs to move to be with me. I never would have asked her, however, because that probably would have meant asking her to leave her career, and sooner or later that would have haunted us both. As much as she loves me, she also loves what she does, and I just could not have taken the responsibility of asking her to move to be with me. It would have been an unfair request, and I know that eventually we would have ended with bitter recriminations. At first, I thought that we just could have continued our previous arrangement: each of us commuted every other weekend to where the other one lived. But finally this was not enough for either of us and it came down to a choice. I didn't want to leave my work, and she really couldn't leave hers since there was no comparable situation where I lived. There are no big orchestras here, and she wouldn't have a chance to be even remotely successful. I think that this is a modern circumstance: she could only do her job in a big city, and I was unwilling to move there. And so, sadly for both of us, we finally broke up.

Many men still cherish traditional masculine dreams of work-related success and accomplishment. The literature dealing with men is filled with discussions of work as a fundamental basis of male self-definition, and most of the men whom I have interviewed do not seem to have renounced their aspirations for career achievement. Such aspirations, however, have become tempered by new realities, and especially by the need to balance career dreams against the need to share work time and house care with one's mate—a source of tension and anxiety for many of us. In addition, it produces feelings that we have somehow not fulfilled the still-present messages about masculinity that we received from our fathers.

Philip, the journalist, provides a good example. He and Joanne both work professionally, and they both take care of the children and the chores at home. Yet, Philip feels that somehow he must make room for his career aspirations and for achievement in traditional ways. "When I go into work my soul gets wound up like a spring," he says:

> I become an emotionally tight person, and this feels fundamentally crazy. I often wonder why I am striving so hard. One could die young from it. You know what it basically has to do with? With being a man! That's what men do: they drive themselves, work hard and die early. I really think that somewhere along the line I was programmed to work this way, to go out and fulfill myself in the world and be useful as a man. My own "programming" wasn't all that conscious. It came, I think, both from my Protestant upbringing and my father's example. He was a lawyer who took on unpopular civil liberties cases, and I've been involved in newspaper and magazine work advocating for social equality and the rights of the poor. This training was never clearly given, however. My father would describe his beliefs and the part played by family traditions, but he never said that I had to follow in his path. There was always a sense of duty to society on both sides of my family. My grandfather worked very hard in business, but he always had a sense of social obligation. Somehow, this got transmitted to me. If I chose to quit and to do nothing for a while, I'd no doubt be seen as a degenerate slob by my family. And also, my wife, Joanne, wouldn't want to do that: she's at the point of really launching her own career and doesn't want to take any time off herself.

A man named William spoke in similar fashion about the legacy of his father and its influence upon a career change which he contemplated. "For quite awhile my work scene has been chaotic," William told me when we initially spoke:

> My job is to develop health-care delivery systems for hospitals, and this pursuit has become very boring for me. I can do it very well and not much challenge remains. I think, in fact, that I'm at a crossroads which seems similar to the one that my father once confronted. He, too, had a job which was boring, which didn't draw on his creativity, but which he kept for the sake of the family, and he was afraid to change. The real conflict, I guess, is how not to play out my father's model and how to make the break. I have a certain amount of fear, a fear that I could actually be happy in redefining my work situation, and I hold myself back by saying that life is not about being happy, but about working hard, and putting up with things. This, I think, is really my father's message, but I seem to have made it my own. What I really want to do, I think, is something that involves working concretely with my hands in a more supportive environment. That goal may sound escapist or crazy, but there it is.

Shortly after this discussion, William opened a shop for bicycle sales and repairs, and thus he converted an avocation into a new line of work. I cannot report, however, that he has now found all the contentment that he seeks, or that he has finally resolved the nagging problems which he associates with his father's example. Such problems often remain, despite the steps that we take to alleviate them.

Relatively new sorts of work issues, however, have arisen for men who must now confront the reality of having women as colleagues or even as superiors. According to researchers, men often experience ambiguous feelings in this regard: we might advocate equality of employment as an abstract formula, but many of us express resentment when job equality actually touches our lives. In the words of writer Anthony Astrachan, men often feel that "women are competent at many jobs . . . and that they deserve equal opportunities to get those jobs. But in their guts (men) don't like working with women who grasp those opportunities."[6] According to some studies, men feel uneasy about being replaced by women on the job when it comes time for promotion, for to admit that a woman could fill one's slot is to admit that one's work is less than valuable. Even more, men feel hesitant about taking directions from a woman, and in addition, men experience a certain level of sexual tension with women at work.[7]

The men I have interviewed, however, are curiously reticent about discussing such concerns. Many state almost by rote that they are in favor of female equality in the workplace and elsewhere. One man told me, for example, "I don't have any trouble working with women, and I even trained a woman to take over my position." When I asked how he would feel if that woman were to become his superior, he was evasive and non-commital. Finally, he noted that such could not occur "because she would never have enough seniority for that." And another man—a T.V. writer—whose new producer is a woman, denied any feelings of resentment or competition. He noted wistfully, however, that "maybe the fact that I have to spend time taking care of my kids has slowed me down in relation to her, since she's unmarried. Maybe I could have done as well as she if I had more time to spend at my job."

I must confess that I, too, am prey to similar feelings. I can readily admit to a sense of ambivalence in apportioning my time between work and house care, but I find great difficulty in confronting my own lingering resistance to the concept that women might be equal at work. If I am backed into a corner, however, these feelings emerge almost of their own accord. When, for example, a woman was hired to replace me in my teaching job, I asserted that she was selected for reasons of gender and to fulfill affirmative action requirements, and I maintained that she was certainly not as competent as I. It took much time before I could acknowledge that I was perhaps mistaken and that my initial response had arisen as much from a wounded male ego as it had from a competitive work attitude. Of course, some men do not resent the job success of women, and others resent anyone's success regardless of sex. Still, secret doubts and resentments have not disappeared even among many of us who claim to believe in the rights and abilities of women in the employment arena.

Even though contemporary men have begun to share and to apportion their work in new ways, older messages and patterns remain important. How do we solve the dilemma of having fulfilling work which does not injure our personal relationships? How can we organize and share in dual-career relationships? How do we deal with traditional messages about work and career that are handed down from family and fathers? How can we cope with our feelings about women and equality in the workplace? We must first realize, I think, that we need not confront these questions in isolation. It is important to recognize that our society is presently undergoing a dramatic economic and social shift, and despite efforts of traditionalists and conservatives to forestall this process, such change will no doubt continue into the future.[8] Women are pursuing careers; men are learning to cope with outmoded models of masculinity. In recognizing that we are not alone, it is helpful to talk about our dilemmas and feelings with other men—our friends and our workmates—and it is also important to discuss our responses with the women in our lives.

We should, in addition, be ready to support these same women in the careers they choose to undertake. These words, of course, constitute merely a slogan until we attempt to put them into practice. Such a commitment might make us review the training and job-based aspirations we have accepted. It might cause us eventually to say goodbye to jobs which no longer accord with personal needs or to ask for serious revision of job requirements. Such revision has been underway at a number of U.S. firms and at such institutions as the Ford Foundation where men recently gained the right to paid paternity leave.[9] We should, in other words, be ready to fight the necessary battles in order to have the best of both worlds—of work and of personal life—without having to sacrifice one world to the other. Although today's climate has momentarily turned in a conservative direction and although some businesses are retrenching to resist campaigns for change, this struggle is still worth the effort.

There is no assurance that it will be easy to heal the divisions and resolve the ambiguities that men currently feel in their work. The efforts we make in this direction will likely be prolonged and without instant reward. The final result, however, will be a manhood based on more clearly achievable aims; it will also open the way to work lives which are coordinated with those of the women that we love. We might have to defer or even renounce our aspirations to be the president of the corporation or a member of the U.S. Senate. In place of such dreams we might discover more gratifying and enjoyable work, a kind of work which more nearly accords with our needs and responsibilities to others and to ourselves.

Notes

1. Levinson, *et al., Seasons of a Man's Life* (New York: Knopf, 1978), pp. 141ff; Sheehy, *Passages: Predictable Crises of Adult Life* (New York: Dutton, 1978), Ch. 5, 8, 15; Gregory Rochlin, *The Masculine Dilemma* (Boston, Little Brown and Co., 1980), pp. 217ff; Erik Erikson, *Childhood and Society* (New York: Norton, 1963), pp. 267–68.
2. See, for example, Daniel Levinson, *et al., Seasons of a Man's Life* (New York: Knopf, 1978), pp. 191ff; Sheehy, *Passages: Predictable Crises of Adult Life* (New York: Dutton, 1978), Chapter 17–20.

3. Richard Sennett and Jonathan Cobb, *The Hidden Injuries of Class* (New York: Vintage, 1972), pp. 74–76, 94–95, 118, 245ff.
4. See George Gilder, *Sexual Suicide* (New York: Bantam, 1973), and *Wealth and Poverty* (New York: Basic Books, 1980).
5. See, for example, Robert and Rhona Rapoport, eds., *Working Couples* (New York: Harper and Row, 1978), especially Chapter 1.
6. Anthony Astrachan, "Men: How They Really Feel About Women Who Work," *Working Woman*, December, 1976, pp. 36–39.
7. See *Ibid.*, also Lynda Lytle Holmstrom, *The Two-Career Family* (Cambridge, Massachusetts: Shenkman Publishing Co., 1973), esp. Chapter 9; Didi Moore, "The Perils of a Two-Income Family," *New York Times Magazine*, September 27, 1981; Mary Bralove, "For Middle-Aged Man A Wife's New Career Upsets Old Balances," *Wall Street Journal*, November 9, 1981.
8. For the historical sources of recent changes in sex roles and family structure, see Donald H. Bell, "Up From Patriarchy: The Male Role in Historical Perspective," Robert Lewis, ed., *Men in Difficult Times: Masculinity Today and Tomorrow* (Englewood Cliffs, New Jersey: Prentice-Hall, 1981), pp. 306–23. See also, Sheila B. Kamerman, *Parenting in an Unresponsive Society: Managing Work and Family* (New York: The Free Press, 1980), pp. 121ff.
9. See, for example, *The New York Times*, March 18, 1981; Bell, "Up From Patriarchy," pp. 322ff; On similar programs in Western Europe and on the comparatively comprehensive efforts of European societies to deal with questions of family policy, see Kamerman, *Parenting in an Unresponsive Society*, Epilogue. See also Ari Korpivaara, "Everything a Father Needs to Know," *Ms. Magazine*, February, 1982, p. 54.

CHAPTER 7

Fathers and Children

One often hears in our society, "If his father had been a different sort of man, then his problems would have been quite different." But it would be even truer to comment also: "if he had been born into a society with a different form of fatherhood . . ."

—MARGARET MEAD, *Male and Female*

Men need their children. . . . In learning to take care of his children's needs, a man learns to take care of his own.

—KRISTINE M. ROSENTHAL AND HARRY F. KESHET, *Fathers Without Partners*

And so we come full circle. Starting as sons, we now become fathers. Once upon a time, a father was consigned to a hospital waiting room, sweating out his children's birth in not-so-splendid isolation. As we grew up, he appeared sometimes as a shadowy and foreboding eminence around the house, or as a weekend pal who taught us baseball or lent us the car. He was mainly the sort of father remembered by men in the opening chapter of this book—competent, rather distant, self-contained—and most of the expert discussion of parenthood was directed entirely toward mothers. Times have indeed changed. Today, a young father is likely to attend monthly pregnancy check-ups and childbirth classes with his wife, to be a partner at the birth of his children, and to take an active and often an equal role in the raising of his sons and daughters. Many fathers today are single parents, and others share joint custody arrangements in a divorce. Such developments have recently been applauded as constituting a step forward. James A. Levine, author of *Who Will Raise the Children?*, a study of alternative parent roles, has quite eloquently noted that, "in nurturing our children, we learn to nurture ourselves. The condition of parenthood is growth."[1] But how do men actually feel about changes in their role as fathers? How do such changes square with our previous images of fatherhood? What inner conflicts and dilemmas do such altered expectations bring about? And, finally, how can the resolution of such dilemmas be seen as an addition to our actual growth and development?

When Rachel and I first decided to have a child we talked seriously about this impending change in our lives and we attempted to conceive a baby for several months. Yet, when she announced one spring day that she had become pregnant, I found myself seized by a wide range of feelings. Elation rapidly gave way to uncertainty, and I wondered with increasing doubt how I could actually be a father. How would I know what to do? Would I suddenly need to think of myself as part of an older generation? I had enough trouble, I realized, just struggling to find myself as a man, and now I was suddenly faced with accepting yet another sense of self. I was no longer to be merely a son, a breadwinner, professional man, and a husband, but a father as well. How could I possibly do all that?

To be sure, Rachel and I had "decided" to have a child, and yet our decision was strongly influenced by the rather indirect pressure of family and society and by our own feelings that it was now "about time" that we became parents. We had been married for nearly five years; we were sometimes questioned by parents and peers about our intentions to have children; many of our contemporaries had become parents, and Rachel and I began to succumb to these subtle (and not-so-subtle) blandishments and injunctions. As in the case of so much else, we were not able to think very clearly about our own priorities and needs, and we attempted to live up to the needs and expectations that we detected in the world around us.

Several other motives played a part in our steps toward parenthood. When we actually began to discuss having a child, Rachel was between jobs, and she thought that this might be a "natural" moment to become a mother. In effect, however, the decision to have a baby gave her both the time and the ability to forstall an eventual and difficult re-evaluation of her career direction. I felt (without really verbalizing such a feeling) that I owed my parents a grandchild, and that I wanted to prove my own virility and masculinity by fathering a child of my own. These were certainly not very positive or clearly chosen reasons for bringing a baby into the world, but in my conversations with other men, I find that similar circumstances recur in explaining why many of us have become fathers. Frequently, we do not seem to choose fatherhood, but we merely decide to "go along for the ride." Such is often the case even when we consciously defer childbearing for careers, a path increasingly followed by numerous couples during the past decade. Even in such circumstances, a set of subtle time pressures come into play: the risk of birth defects increases significantly for women in their thirties, and recent research indicates that the father's age might be a significant factor as well.[2] The decision to have children thus seems to creep up on men and women who have devoted their early adulthood to establishing themselves in professions and careers. When to bear children often remains a problematical question, whether we come to it early or late.

Rachel and I quickly discovered that actually becoming parents was not a simple matter. Months passed, and we were not able to conceive. She became worried; I felt shaken by this threat to my sense of masculine self-esteem. After all, in biological terms the primary male function is to father children, and it seemed to me that becoming a father would serve as a necessary emblem of my own manhood. Hadn't I done most of the things expected of a man? I had played football, established a career, married, become a tax-paying citizen. Now it appeared that I was unable to father a child! I shuddered with anxiety when by chance I ran across a newspaper article discussing a supposed decline in the average sperm count of American men; I looked with envy and anguish at men who took their kids for walks or played with them in the park; sometimes I was not able to face these feelings of dread, and I then struggled to deny their very existence. For several months, I thought to myself that the joys of fatherhood were pleasures from which I would be forever barred.

Such remorse and upset was premature. In speaking with friends and consulting with our family physician, Rachel and I discovered that, in fact, it sometimes took months to conceive a baby. I guess that she and I had expected that any lovemaking without benefit of contraception would almost automatically lead to pregnancy (a belief that ironically resulted from long years of worry about actually getting pregnant). Finally, however, the proper symptoms began to appear—a missed period, fatigue, the beginning of morning sickness—and a visit to the gynecologist confirmed our suspicions: Rachel was indeed pregnant; we would most likely be parents, and I could discard anxieties about not fulfilling my manly role. What a relief! And yet what a burden! I would be a father and would prove to the world that I was indeed a man. And yet, as I was then but dimly aware, being a father would dramatically change my life.[3]

In my discussion with men, I have found that becoming a father completes an important passage in our lives, a passage which we often take as evidence for our capability and standing as men. Such a time is a most anxious one to the male ego. We are worried that we will not be able to conceive children; we are worried that we will conceive them and this will alter our lives; we want to be supportive of our mates in their own anxieties, and yet we often tend to withdraw into worries and anxieties of our own. Men today, as we have seen, harbor contradictory and ambiguous emotions about many aspects and events in their lives. The question of childbearing and fatherhood is the source of some of our deepest anxieties and some of our most profoundly divided feelings. In becoming fathers we fulfill perhaps the most typical and traditional male function. Yet, we are also faced with the need to harmonize our conventional images about being a man with whatever new and altered sense we have of ourselves. Fatherhood is an event which can call into question our most conscious and careful resolutions about acting in new and non-sexist ways. As fathers we must contend not only with past images of masculinity, but with present resolutions about change and equality, and with hopes for the future of ourselves and our children. Fatherhood is the point at which many of our contradictory and ambivalent feelings seem to converge.

Rachel and I became expectant parents during the late 1960's, and although this was a time of awakening consciousness about sex-role behavior, I did not yet think that it was a man's place to attend the monthly pregnancy check-ups in the doctor's office or to be very involved in early preparation for motherhood. This may be one of the most important tasks that the expectant father can fulfill.[4] During pregnancy, women's bodies are constantly changing; their emotions undergo wide swings. Men, in contrast, witness such changes more indirectly. We watch as our wives become rounder in figure, as they seek to meet their dietary requirements, as they try to eliminate smoking and drinking from their lives; and we react with pleasure to the first signs of a fetal heartbeat or to reports of the first fetal kicks. Women at this time need our support for the sacrifices that they must make and for the physical and emotional changes that they experience. We can help by preparing meals, monitoring calories and grams of protein, cutting down on our own indulgence in alcohol or tobacco (in order to spread the discomfort of renunciation), and by attending physician's appointments and eventually childbirth classes with our wives.

Some time in her second trimester, however, Rachel began to fear that our child would be born with deformities, and I began to share in her fears as well. According to physicians and childbirth experts, such anxieties are a typical concern for expectant parents.[5] Some of these fears are well-founded—birth defects *do* occasionally occur—and some are less than rational. Rachel and I had always been able to exert a modicum of control over our surrounding environment and over the major events in our lives. Now, however, we were faced with an occurrence over which we could exert scant influence. This baby would be born almost regardless of what we did to affect the pregnancy and delivery. It would be a separate individual and there were not many ways that we could control its size, shape, or health. Instead of welcoming the mystery in this process, we both seized upon its indeterminacy, and we became fearful. Perhaps our fear that our child would embody our own buried and unconscious selves was what really emerged in Rachel's recurring nightmares and my own recurring anxieties. Perhaps we shared more acutely than most in the universal phenomenon of apprehension and stage-fright brought on by the nine-month process of waiting. At Jake's birth, as we shall see, these fears led to an unexpected and rather humorous reaction.

The Lamaze method of prepared birth had just begun to gain wide acceptance, and we decided that, if at all possible, Rachel would bear our child without anesthesia, and I would be present in the delivery room. Fathers have since gained ready acceptance as attendants at the birth of their own children,[6] but in those days—little more than a decade ago—the presence of a father was seen as rather novel. As I recall, we had to provide at our own expense a registered nurse who served only to administer to the father if he were to faint or become overwhelmed at the sight of the delivery—a far-fetched possibility, as the subsequent success of "natural" childbirth methods have shown.

The Lamaze childbirth classes had acquainted us with the various stages of the birth process and had taught us breathing exercises with which to overcome the pain of labor contractions. On the night of Jake's birth Rachel moved very rapidly through the first portion of the delivery process, talking and joking between contractions, and she was then wheeled into the delivery room for the birth itself. At each contraction I breathed along with her, pacing her as if we were running a marathon together. Although pushing out an infant proved to be exceedingly hard work, Rachel was able to gather her strength between contractions and to apply new effort to every push. As Jake began to emerge from the womb, I felt the sense of elation and joy which other men have typically reported.[7] This was unlike anything I had ever experienced: a fact of nature like a volcano or a tidal wave; nothing could stand in its way. The appointed hour had arrived and Jake would be born no matter what else took place in the world. I was in awe and shock, and yet as Jake came forth I experienced an odd sense of confusion. I forgot the lessons of childbirth class which indicated that the baby is normally turned face downward as it comes into the world, and that therefore one usually first sees the top and back of its head. Suddenly, I became panicked: seeing the back of his head, I immediately thought that this baby had no face at all! How could a child live without a face? What would he be like at age forty if he had no defining features? All the months of anxiety about birth defects and deformities seemed to meet their self-fulfilling conclusion. My child seemed to be without a face! We were right all along in our worry! Just then, however, Jacob turned on his side, and I could clearly see an ear. "At least this baby has an ear," I thought. "Things can't be quite as bad as I had imagined." Suddenly he rolled over completely and a fully formed and beautiful (although somewhat wrinkled) face emerged. "Hooray! He has a nose and eyes and a mouth! He's a real person! He's going to be all right!" A moment later he drew his first breath and began to squall with shock and amazement and perhaps with rage at being taken from his warm and dark surroundings into the cold and bright world. "It's Jacob," I suddenly realized. "It's Jacob, my son."

Other men also confess some unexpected reactions. "I found myself crying throughout the entire birth process," one man told me. "I was scared because the fetal monitor showed that the baby's heartbeat had slowed down, but even more, I was overwhelmed by the power of the event itself. My wife was so vital and strong in pushing the baby out that I felt overcome by just witnessing her. I wasn't really sobbing, but I just had tears pouring down my cheeks, and I sometimes had to turn away and to shield myself from the intensity of the experience. Finally, when the baby was born, my fears were allayed because it was obvious once they had worked her over a bit and suctioned mucus out of her lungs, that she would be OK. The three of us then spent a long time together in the birthing room, and that was wonderful. I was overcome with feelings for both my wife and my baby." And another man tells me about the way in which he dealt with some of his emotions. "The various key moments of childbearing really give you a high," he says. "Finding out that my wife was pregnant, hearing the heartbeat, were instances of this kind and the birth was the highest moment of them all. But at the same time," he adds, "I found myself resisting these moments: they entailed a loss of control and a loss of defenses. They were moments of mixed emotions, and they were frightening as well as joyous. At first I withdrew at times, but in the course of the pregnancy I learned how to let it just happen—it felt scary, but mainly I just let go of my defensive feelings. When I would begin to feel a sense of ambivalence and I wanted to hold my emotions back, I began to say, 'Well, I can go with this; it's going to be all right.' By the time of the birth, this was how I had begun to react."

Classes about childbirth helped prepare me and other men for the actual delivery, but not for what was to follow. As are many of us, I was bereft of lessons about how to be a father, and I lacked useful models from the past. Our own fathers had done well enough in their way. They had occasionally changed diapers or prepared dinners, but they provided us with no consistent patterns (nor could they) for sharing these strong emotions regularly or for attempting to be equal partners with wives in the process of parenting. The problem lay not only in the mere physical functions of parenthood—one could eventually learn to feed or attend to a baby, clean the house or take wash to the Laundromat. The difficulty lay even more in the need to redefine our expected roles. I had slowly worked to be an equal partner with Rachel and had wrestled with whatever threat I had experienced to my sense of masculine self-esteem. Now I was asked to take on much more responsibility, to surrender more of my work time, to re-order my schedule, to do more housework, to earn the income, and to give emotional support in order to help withstand the inevitable onset of maternal post-birth depression. All of this, I felt, was more than I had bargained for. How could I fulfill all these expectations? My father did not need to do all this when I was born, and many of my friends did not seem faced by so many tasks and pressures. Friends, however, who were thus confronted, appeared reluctant to talk about their feelings (possibly in the belief that silence would allow them better to cope), and even those with whom I met regularly in my men's group were not very communicative about the pressures and changes which fatherhood had brought into their lives.

I believe that today one of the greatest needs we face as men and as potential fathers is to share knowledge of the post-partum process and an understanding of the contradictory and difficult feelings that it involves. This is a time of great turmoil for both husbands and wives. It is also a time which is little understood by parents as well as by researchers. A good bit of investigation has recently focused on the ways nurturant fathers can influence their children, and some research has also indicated that increased child care might have positive effects upon fathers, helping them, in the words of psychologist Ross D. Parke, "to become more expressive and gentle in their relationships with other people." But as Parke also notes, very little is actually known about the ways that men change after becoming fathers.[8] Nor, we must add, is much known about the ways that men feel about new parenthood, about the changes in male self-conception that this brings about, and about the stresses it involves. Further investigation of such questions is important; it is also important that men have a sense of freedom to share their feelings and that they devise some collective ways to assist in meeting the inevitable changes that fathering entails.

In becoming a new father, I faced a series of issues which I felt hesitant to discuss for fear of revealing what I supposed was my incapacity as a parent and what I also took to be a deeply irrational side of my nature. Initially, I felt a reluctance to actually hold my new son, and an abiding fear that he might drop out of my arms and break upon the floor. It is possible, of course, that my fears might have stemmed from some deep-seated hostility aroused by the new situation in which I found myself,[9] but it is perhaps too facile to attribute my anxiety simply to such feelings of anger. Even more, I had a strong intuition that I was just unready for parenthood, and that I did not really know how to hold a baby, to cradle him firmly in my arms to quiet his fears and to transmit love and security by my touch.

I could not bear, in addition, the thought of leaving Jake alone. This was a fear which Rachel and I both shared, and we would go to him at the least provocation: when his diaper might be wet or when he seemed hungry, of course, but also whenever he cried, whether resisting his nap or awakening in the middle of the night. A certain amount of care in this regard is important: too much parental concern is probably better than not enough, and feeding when the baby is in need seems more beneficial than a scheduled and rigid regimen. Other fathers tell me about similar fears of leaving their infants alone and of the pressing desire to comfort and protect their children from all manner of imaginary harm. In the literature on parenting, fathers are supposedly the prime supporters of the independence and curiosity of their infants and toddlers.[10] In my own experience, however, and in that of many of my informants, fathers often seem to be fearful and overly protective. We want to support the explorations and curiosity of our children (especially our sons), and yet we often want to shield our children from their own attempts at independence. This seems but one of the myriad ways in which men are suspended between rival sets of feelings. Such suspension, in fact, seems scarcely alleviated with the passage of time. Jake is now a pre-adolescent. When he mounts his bicycle to ride off into the sunset, I still find myself asking him about his destination, telling him exactly when to return, and warning him about riding on busy streets. There is not such a long step between my present solicitousness and my earlier need to respond to his every infant cry.

When Jake began to crawl, I found myself having to know at all moments where he was headed, and I imagined that he was playing with electric sockets or that he was about to fall down the stairs. I checked each night to see that he was properly tucked into his bed and that he was still breathing. Fear of sudden infant crib death (a much publicized tragedy) was always in my mind, and it was years before I realized that Jake would probably not expire from that particular malady. Of course, one might dismiss these fears as the product of an overwrought and obsessive imagination. I am willing to acknowledge such assessments. And yet, my conversations with new fathers has revealed similar fears and anxieties. We might not all check to see if our children are still breathing in their beds, and some of us might be less solicitous and protective than others, but I am surprised at the frequency with which fathers report such feelings and the degree with which we wrestle with (or surrender to) our irrational fears. Surely, these specters that haunt us can be somewhat exorcised by a resolve to share them with each other.

One new father told me, for example, about some of his concerns for his newborn son and of how he attempts to master them. "I worry about a lot of things: about our dog suddenly attacking the baby out of jealousy, for example, and about crib death. At first, I went in to check on him all the time, but I don't do that as much any more. I don't see it as something that I can really control. Mainly, I would like to believe that this kid is going to survive, given the minimum of care and love. There is no way of avoiding terrible freak accidents or some rare disease; you have to consider that as a possibility, because it happens all the time, but it's not something that you can really prevent by compulsively asserting control."

Another new father told me about some feelings toward his infant daughter and of how these emotions sometimes emerge. "Although I'm pretty calm about handling the baby," this father says, "I'm afraid sometimes that I might drop her or that I might hurt her when I change her diaper. The other day I actually did jab her with a pin when I was changing a diaper and at first I was really surprised. I had prided myself on being sort of an expert with the diapers and I thought I had worked out a kind of fail-safe system where nothing could go wrong. I happened to catch a little roll of her skin and I jabbed it in there. She cried non-stop for about two hours after that, and it was an excruciating experience for all of us."

This man then related some of his understanding of the event:

> I began to think at this point that I might really be harboring some secret anger toward the baby. Before she was born, I used to joke in rather sadistic ways about birth defects or about child abuse, and finally my wife asked me about why I did this. I came to realize that it was my way of ridding myself through humor of the fantasies which I carried around and couldn't verbalize in any other manner. I feel that I'm fundamentally a gentle person, and that I don't really act on my aggressive fantasies. Basically, I've come to understand that these are fairly primitive feelings against the baby for displacing me. For a man, having a baby entails being denied a certain sense of specialness, and it means losing out as the center of attention. My wife naturally gives most of her energy to the baby, and I was afraid of this during the pregnancy when I joked about it, and I guess that I'm afraid of it still. And in the middle of everything I seem to have jabbed the baby with a pin! I think that I understand my feelings in some way but I have to say that I am a bit amazed at myself. My relations with the baby—even though I love her—seem sometimes to take on the quality of a secret war within the household.

Among the most difficult aspects of contemporary fatherhood is the increased demand on our time and energy brought about by new expectations for the sharing of child care. Until Jake went to kindergarten I found myself staying home with him at least two full days during the week. Since my job as a college teacher permitted me a flexible time schedule, I watched him in the mornings or I sometimes took him to a cooperative play group for part of the day (and I often shared with other parents—mostly mothers—in the activities of the group). For the rest of those days he and I were mostly together. I remember mornings which dawned with the sky full of rain or snow, an ominous sign that we two would be cooped up at home while Rachel went out to her work. When Jake began to crawl and then to toddle around the house and it seemed that he got into every drawer and cabinet, I soon found that I did not have a moment to myself in the attempt to keep up with him. I experienced the age-old frustration common to mothers and to housewives (and the newer frustration of the househusband). At those moments I remembered the laconic note of caution provided by a close friend, the father of two pre-schoolers, shortly before Jake's birth. When I asked him what I could expect in having a child, his only response was, "Wait and see: it will change your life." Prophetic words! As one recent father told me, "Having an infant is like nothing in the world. It's more work than anyone expects or than can be explained. I just never thought I'd be doing this as a man."

I do not wish to portray either contemporary fatherhood or the sharing of child care in a negative light. Although being a father under today's changed circumstances is a demanding task, the rewards are great. At the very least, we can be closer to our children than were most fathers of an earlier generation, and we can also have the satisfaction of learning that we as men can become competent in a variety of ways—not only in our careers and work, but in our capabilities for nurturance. I think that my early years of sharing in Jake's care has woven an indissoluable bond between him and me. Despite a divorce and the fact that Jake and I now live most of the year nearly a continent apart, we remain tightly linked through feelings of love and mutual care. Since I was not merely a traditional father to my son, I did not fade into the background when the initial nuclear family bonds were broken. I was a fully equal parent, and, as such, I tried to maintain my primary connection with him regardless of the changes in the relationship between his mother and me. Although the experience of divorce was painful, I believe that Jake now feels good that he has retained the love and care of both parents, and that I have worked to maintain my place as his father. As he told me, "There's not a lot that I want to change about you, Dad. Maybe you worry a little too much, but it makes me feel that you really love me. I think that you're just about the idealest father I know." Of course, Jake might feel that he is obligated to tell me such things. Still I hope (and I think) that he really means what he says.

In speaking with other men about fatherhood, I've come to understand more about the two-sided quality of our experience—our joy at sharing in the care of children and our misgivings at how this might affect our self-concept as men. As we have seen, the new lessons of manhood do not come easily and each of them elicits a price in terms of earlier ideas about masculine identity. For example, Marty says this concerning his new parental responsibilities and his feelings about them:

> Clearly, the fact that I have taken on so much of the child care in the family is a statement about the role of the male and how it is different now than it used to be. It's something that at times I resent. I don't like having to hold a full-time job and to do child care for half my remaining time. Our son, Jonathan, goes to someone's house two mornings a week, and then we have a play group with other couples for three mornings, but when my wife, Marsha, and I take care of Jonathan, we split it evenly, and I feel upset that I also have to work a full forty hour week and that she's only working a part-time job. Sometimes I also feel bad that I have to undertake housekeeping tasks like cooking and cleaning for part of the time. There are moments when I really resent having to do more than my own father did and more than I thought I would do when I was growing up. I don't come home and have a drink and put my feet up and read a paper. I come home and take out the garbage and make my son dinner. Then I help with the dinner for us, and then I bathe him and I help put him to bed.
>
> As you can see, I have ambivalent feelings about all of this. I often feel disconcerted and even angry about sharing more than is expected from the vast majority of men. Sometimes I even resent other men at the hospital where I work. Men my age—in their early thirties—have more time to do the same amount of professional work. When I compare myself to them I feel sometimes that I have a bad deal.

Marty allows, however, that there are many positive aspects to his experience. "First, there's someone else—my wife—who gets to do other things besides child care. I think that my relationship with Marsha is a lot better than it would be if she were a mother full time.

She's an active, exciting person who is intellectually and emotionally alive and all of these things are encouraged by the agreement we have, and so our experience together is much fuller."

"I think," Marty adds, "that I am closer with Jonathan than I might have been, and that's a wonderful thing. Somehow, kids help to allay one's 'existential dilemmas': the worries about what we are doing with our lives, and why we don't do something else. Kids have to be taken care of; their everyday lives are so meaningful, as are the big changes that they go through in learning to talk, and walk, and to negotiate in the world. It's true, as well, that the love you get back from them is so fulfilling, and so rich. Their dependency on you is very meaningful, and it's more than just having your time taken up. The love that they give back is just unbelievably gratifying."

"I feel," a man named Steve tells me, "that I'm much closer physically to my two-year-old son than my father was to me. I really love to hold Luke. We take baths together a lot, and I love to smell him, and to hug him, and to kiss him. It's hard for me to imagine that my father ever related to me in that way. Certainly, he didn't in my conscious memory. I'm sure that Luke and I will go through phases when such visible closeness is taboo, but now it isn't, and that's really nice."

"Besides giving Luke baths," Steve says, "I dance with him, either with me holding him or with him running around. He really loves to dance, and this is a legitimate opportunity for me to act like a kid and to express myself in ways in which I normally find difficult. When I'm with him I can allow myself to behave in ways that otherwise might just seem weird."

"Finally," Steve continues, "I would like to be able to give Luke real confidence in himself. I think right now that he's the greatest kid in the world. It's easy to say, of course, that most people really feel that way about their kids, but I'm not sure that most people transmit that understanding. My own father didn't give me that feeling. His approval seemed always to be conditional on my performance. No matter what my own son decided to do with his life, I would like him just to be able to feel that he was all right."

Recent investigations have shown that, in fact, men make a particular contribution to the development of their children. Fathers tend to play in more physical and vigorous ways with their children than do mothers (Steve's dancing with Luke is a good example). Although fathers who serve as primary caretakers sometimes adopt the verbal and cognitive styles of play most common to mothers, studies show that they usually maintain their more intensely physical and active modes of play, as well. Men treat sons and daughters somewhat differently, however. They seem to play more intensely with boy children and for longer periods of time, while they tend to express more overt affection for daughters and to hold them more closely and protectively. This tends to reinforce differences between boys and girls, and as one researcher has commented, "This pattern . . . may be the earliest form of sex role typing."[11]

The contrasting ways that fathers and mothers relate to their children seem to make an important difference in the development of the child. Researchers have found that even at an early age children who have had substantial interaction with their fathers tend to be friendlier to adults in general. This is especially the case with boys, but a father who is supportive and nurturant can have a real impact on the ability of daughters to interact with the outside world. Some recent studies indicate that children who have been raised equally by fathers and mothers or by fathers alone seem to show greater confidence in their capacity to control the surrounding environment.[12] Ultimately, such a belief can help enhance achievement in later life. Fathers, in other words, are important, and the change in the relationship of a father and a mother or a decline in the quality and the frequency of fathering can have a pronounced effect on a young child.

When Rachel and I decided to end our marriage, I was aware that this would drastically affect my relationship with Jacob. Although at odds with each other, Rachel and I were both concerned with finding ways to lessen the impact of our separation on Jake and to make arrangements which might ensure some continuity in his life. Such a seemingly objective statement, however, greatly distorts our turmoil and the dilemma which confronted us, as it does that of other couples who find themselves in similar circumstances. After all, Rachel and I could no longer speak together in any but the most angry terms, and we could scarcely stand (at least during the initial time of separation) to be together in the same room. And yet we mostly did not transmit our anger and hostility to our son, and thus he was injured less by the situation of growing estrangement than he otherwise might have been. The battle was between Rachel and me, and we thankfully refrained from asking Jacob to choose sides between us. Jake, for his part, railed against both of his parents, hitting and kicking us when we told him of our decision to separate, and later attempting physically to draw us back together. These are strategies which are typical of children in the throes of separation and divorce, and (as was the case with Jake) these strategies for bringing parental reconciliation are mostly doomed to failure.

When Rachel and I finally separated, I decided that it would be both unfair and absurd to give up custody of my son and to become a "weekend father." After all, Jacob had been brought up almost equally by the two of us, and both of us felt that we were competent to provide for his care. At first, Rachel and I hit upon what we thought was a novel plan (but I have since learned that numerous estranged couples employ a similar arrangement to ease their time of transition). Instead of one or the other of us moving permanently out of the house (usually the role of the father in marital separation) we decided that we each would be present in the house for half a week, and for the rest of the time we would maintain a separate residence. In this way Jacob got to remain at home while Rachel and I alternated our time with him and worked to retain some vestiges of shared parenthood.

Such an arrangement lasted for only several months, however. We both found that as good as it might be for Jake, this plan seriously hindered us from building new lives for ourselves. Thus began another phase of our growing separation. Rachel and I found new apartments which were in close proximity to each other. Jacob now came to my place for four days a week and to Rachel's for three days, and we reversed this schedule in the following week. This was a better situation for both parents, but in the long run it was not as good for the child, for as soon as he had established himself at one apartment, it was time for him to return to that of his other parent.

It seems likely that the separation and divorce of parents might in many cases be in the best interest of children. It often allows them to shift from a situation of domestic turmoil to one of relative calm. Still, a parental estrangement remains a difficult experience for children, in emotional as well as physical and material terms. For a long time Jacob was fundamentally sad that his parents were no longer living together and in his fantasies he felt guilty for having in some way caused our separation. He also had a good bit of resentment at being asked to move from one apartment to another and at needing to fulfill the differing expectations that his mother and I now placed upon him. Rachel and I had watched our marriage come apart because our values and expectations had begun to diverge. They often diverged, as well, in terms of such relatively simple matters as Jacob's bed time, how often he cleaned his room, and how much television he got to watch.

Our new situation did not go smoothly in other ways, as well. Rachel and I were both attempting to re-establish our lives and this meant that we saw new people and that we took more time for ourselves and our immediate needs. Thus, Rachel sometimes asked me to keep Jake at my house for more than my allotted days, and I asked her to do the same. This was a constant source of friction, and often I found myself stifling an upsurge of anger, not wanting to chance a renewal of hostilities and the further disruption of our still-fragile agreement. I would sometimes conclude a particularly difficult telephone conversation with Rachel, and I would then rail against Sara, who had come to visit at my apartment, or I would descend into a despairing mood for the remainder of the day. Separation and divorce are moments in which one's emotions vary enormously and in which our feelings unpredictably change. We still remain attached to our former spouse while we also seek to break that attachment and to free ourselves from our earlier commitments and emotional allegiances.

After the first months of separation I slowly began to experience a new stability in my life, and I moved into the increasingly common situation of the single father—spending a good bit of time alone with my son and responsible for his care.[13] There came a day, however, when Rachel and I entered into still another stage in our revised relationship. She had, I knew, been seeing a man who lived in another part of the country, and she now announced that she was moving there to be with him and that she wanted to take Jake along. I was both astounded and shaken by this news. Seemingly, the last vestige of my former life was to be stripped away. Even though Rachel was Jake's mother, she was not his sole and primary parent and I responded with intense anger. I threatened a court order forbidding her to take him out of the state; I swore that I would fight for custody; I vowed to establish my rights as a father.

A visit to an attorney helped to put my anger in perspective. This lawyer, a woman who had handled many divorce cases, told me that to be sure, fathers were today winning a greater number of custody suits, and that courts had slowly begun not to presume that the mother was automatically the more capable parent.[14] A court fight between Rachel and me, however, would no doubt be long, costly, and emotionally disastrous. I would probably need to ask Jacob to testify that his mother was unfit. We might have to go through a long process of appeal which would entail pain for all of us and especially for Jake. In fact, Rachel was anything but unfit. She had been a good mother to Jacob (as she today continues to be), and our disagreements over his care were not over fundamental questions of parenthood but over the varying styles which she and I had increasingly adopted. In addition, Jacob would be deeply hurt by having to speak against one or the other of his parents. Wouldn't it be better, my attorney asked, to work to heal old wounds rather than to open new ones? Wouldn't it be in Jake's interest to let him go with his mother and not to poison whatever relationship the three of us still had together? After all, one is not really definitively divorced when one shares a child with another person. There is always a relationship to maintain in regard to the child's upbringing.

After some contemplation and much sadness, I came to see the wisdom of my attorney's advice. We would conclude a joint custody agreement which in fact acknowledged that Rachel would take Jake to her new residence, and that he would live with me during school vacations. At some future time, perhaps, Rachel and I would agree to alter this plan and Jake would come to live with me on a more regular basis. I felt that I had surrendered a great deal, and that I had given up a part of my psyche and my soul. I had lost my marriage and now I feared for the loss of my child.

Since that time, Jacob and I have come to stabilize our relationship on a new footing. I speak with him every week on the telephone and I take part at least vicariously, in all the major events of his life—his triumphs and tragedies at school, his Little League games, his upsets and his joys. When vacation time rolls around, he gets on an airplane and flies to meet me. After some initial moments while I marvel at how tall he has grown, and while we both seek to overcome our feelings of awkwardness and discomfort, we begin to move into growing harmony. When we are apart there are moments when I feel a kind of anguished longing to be with him and when I feel abused and upset by the strange turn which my life has taken. But all of this vanishes when Jake finally emerges from the airplane.

For the first year or two of this arrangement, its difficulties were pronounced. During his vacation, Jacob would get the urge to talk at length on the telephone with his mother to bridge his distance from her and to assuage his sense of guilt for perhaps abandoning her to be with me. He has recently been able to speak openly about these feelings, and as he told me, "I'm now more used to this arrangement. I don't really like to change from one house to the next, but I think that it is getting easier as I get older."

Many issues remain. I miss out on Jake's day-to-day growth and development. He has to adjust to life in two very different places and two different climes. His mother and I are both without him for long periods and he cannot be with school friends during vacations. There is also the financial burden of maintaining this sort of long distance relationship in which the only real winners are the airlines. In addition, since both Rachel and I have now remarried, Jacob must adjust to the different patterns of life in two homes and to the varying expectations of his parents and stepparents. But as he somewhat humorously explains, he can now find at least one of the four adults who will see things his way and will accede to his needs. Although he might actually be making the best of a bad thing, Jacob has found some ways to adjust to a situation which is not an easy one. Despite my own sadness at his absence and some vestiges of anger at Rachel for taking him from me, I, too, have found that this is a workable arrangement that contains some advantages. Instead of being a part-time father, I am a full-time father for part of the time. I am with my son for long enough periods to insure that we have a growing relationship with each other. I do not now feel like the divorced father who has been cut off from his child, but a man who happens to have a son who lives with him for part of the year. If my experience might not be an example for all divorced fathers in their changed relationships with their children, it might stand as one among the many ways in which contemporary men are attempting to maintain their roles as fathers in the face of alterations in their personal and family lives.

One man, for example, told me of a similar post-divorce experience and how his relationship with his six-year-old son eventually began to stabilize. "I feel now as if I gained a child instead of losing one," he says, "and this has been one of the most wonderful and surprising gifts. Instead of being a second parent—which I essentially was in my marriage—now I'm the first parent in the time we are together. This has been a real discovery for both of us. It isn't as good as it was before, but in some ways it is better than it ever was."

"My son and I have our fights," this man relates. "Mostly these take place when I am going to bring him back to his mother. Recently, for example, I had a speech to write and a conference to organize, and I also had three kids to take care of on a Sunday afternoon—my son and two friends. I was trying to do everything at once, and I felt pulled in all directions. By the end of the day I was very tense and I yelled at him to hurry up and pack his bag so he could go back to his mother's house. And then suddenly I stopped, and I was able to tell him that I was feeling upset that he was leaving and going back to Mommy's. I told him that he hadn't done anything wrong at all and that I loved him very much. We both felt easier after that and that whole episode was a real positive step for me as a father. In a way, I have been engaged in a process of learning to be a father by means of the divorce, something that I never thought would happen."

In a like manner, Stan, to whom we have often referred, tells me about maintaining the love of his children throughout his process of marital reorganization. "One thing that I know about my two sons," he says, "is that I'll always love them and that they'll love me. In this respect, having them feels like the other strong family relationships in my life: those with my mother and grandmother. Time might pass, but we can just jump right back into a relationship together and we can start up from where we left off."

"My current arrangement is that I see the kids on Monday or Tuesday afternoon, and when they leave it's always a little hard to let go of them, but we work it out because we expect this separation. By midweek I begin to miss them again, and then they come on Friday night and sometimes they stay the weekend. After the weekend is over I just hate to see them go back to their mother's house. By then, they actually *want* to go back to their mother, and this really hurts me. I'd really like for them to say that they want to stay here all the time: it's part of needing to maintain my primary relationship with them and needing them to love me. At those moments I feel pulled by many emotions: love, resignation, anger, the beginnings of letting go so that we can say goodbye. I get depressed, and this lasts in some mild form until they show up again at the start of the week."

In reflecting on some of these issues, the attorney Andy Brown notes that he has learned from his own altered relationship with his son how to be a different parent than was his own father.

> When I was going through the initial separation, I had doubts about being available to Michael and being able to provide for him. I equated

it with financial responsibility, but this issue really entailed much more than that. It raised the question of whether I could be different from my own father. Was I going to be a drop-out father in the way that my father was with me? This worry really got to me during the time of the initial separation. Finally, in order to overcome those fears, I attempted very consciously to pay as much attention as I could to Michael, even driving long distances to be with him in the new place that he and his mother were living.

When she and I eventually made a decision to get a divorce I just totally broke down and cried over the sadness of the loss and over the worry that this somehow would end my relationship with my son. But at this moment I also realized that I was a responsible person and that I could care for Michael. I knew that I had been a good father and that I could do things differently than my own father. It took the actual divorce agreement to release these feelings. As painful as this moment was, it was probably one of the most enlightening moments of my life. I realized that I really was a father, and that I could be one, and that I indeed *am* one. Not long after that I decided to move permanently to where my ex-wife was living in order to see my son on a steady basis.

Divorce and separation raise a number of other difficulties for us as parents. Not the least of these problems is the need to adjust to the children of the women with whom me might form new relationships, or their need to adjust to our own children. Being a stepparent has always been a problematical undertaking, and it is a present-day concern for men who have experienced divorce, separation, and a revision in their family roles. As Stan notes about his new post-divorce arrangement, "All this constant coming and going, this on-again, off-again relationship with my sons takes its toll on my attempts to build a solid connection with Amy, the woman I'm now seeing. She tries to give me support when I feel depressed, and she attempts to adjust to the constant arrivals and departures, but it's difficult for her. She gets jealous at times when the kids seem to cut into our life together, and also when it's clear that I want to be with them more than her. Often, when they are about to leave she and I don't really have a relationship with each other, since I'm so absorbed with the boys. This situation really pulls me in lots of ways: between my children and the woman I love."

Jack Cohen, the novelist, tells me about his experience with the children of women he saw after his marital separation. "When I first broke up with my wife, I met a woman to whom I was very attracted.

She was divorced and I was separated, and I started to have a relationship with her. And the thing that more than anything else made me feel absolutely numb—in fact, I got impotent with her and couldn't get it up to have sex—was her kids. It only happened one time, but it made me realize that the whole situation was impossible. She had four children ranging in age from five to fifteen, and I didn't like any of them. I was really surprised because I usually like kids, but my feelings about them and how they treated her were enough to sour our whole relationship."

"Tommy, the son of the woman I'm seeing now is an all-right kid," Jack says, "but it's hard to imagine living with her because of him. The impediment is not just that she has a child, but that she has a kid that is used to being the star of his single-parent home, and who is now uncomfortable in seeing me take his mother's time and attention. He gets very negative sometimes, and I can't stand him when he becomes moody and resistant like that. I guess that this isn't an unusual situation. Lots of men and women face it, and I guess that she and I could work it out if we tried, but attempting to live in the same house with Tommy until he went off to college would really be difficult."

Sara, Jacob, and I have confronted some similar issues in learning to live together. Initially Jacob was reluctant to show Sara much about his feelings, and he maintained his distance from her. He would not respond to her requests that he be responsible for picking up after himself or that he take part in household chores. With the passage of time and after much discussion, we began to understand the needs that we each had. Sara came to see that Jake felt her an interloper in his mother's place, but she did not give up her attempts to nurture and support him while she continued to request that he do his share around the house. Jake, for his part, came to accept the likelihood that Rachel and I would not get back together again, and that Sara's presence seemed to be rather permanent. I, myself, worked to be as clear as I could with both of the people that I loved, and I attempted not to play the role of mediator between them, the unwitting lynchpin, as it were, of our new triangular family relationship. I sometimes still found myself carrying messages back and forth, asking Jacob to set the table or to clean his room or telling Sara about Jake's feelings and anger.

The times when Jacob arrived from his mother's house were particularly difficult, and although we now have followed the same schedule for several years, these moments still produce much tension. It takes a special effort to adjust to the changed schedule that a pre-adolescent brings to our life, to the loss of privacy that his arrival entails, to the need to cook more dinners and lunches, and to the inability for Sara and me to be alone together. She and I experience a certain estrangement for several days before Jake moves back into the house, and we both dread the changes which the arrival of the third household member will bring. The old conflicts sometimes flare up, and I again discover myself pulled between Sara and Jacob, attempting to give time and love to both. It would be best, of course, to bring these persisting disagreements into the open, where we might then resolve them, but it is hard for me to face the possibility of struggle between the two main people in my life. I often conclude that it is better to disregard conflict and to avoid negative feelings: this a particular legacy of the past and of my upbringing as a man. By now I have learned to question such aversion to the discussion of feelings, but I still sometimes find myself helpless to act in accordance with my new knowledge.

Nor is the situation an easy one for Jacob. As he has noted, he must confront a differing set of expectations in each of the two households in which he lives, his mother's and mine, and he must face a readjustment to these expectations several times a year. "Both sets of my parents are real nice to me," he says, "but they are different from each other. At one house I have a routine to get used to, and at the other house I have to get used to not having this routine. At one place my stepparent gives me directions and at the other place the stepparent expects my real parent to do this. The rules of one family are tight in some ways and loose in others and it's just the opposite with the other family. Once I get to either place for awhile it's O.K., but it's hard to get used to both."

If such situations are difficult for children, they also are difficult for parents. Learning to assume new responsibilities for parenthood is a task which confronts men today in homes unaffected by separation and divorce. In households headed by single and divorced fathers, these questions have become all the more pressing. Such fathers must work especially hard to maintain and build their commitments to their children. In addition, they are faced with launching new relationships with women and with harmonizing the connections between these potential mates and their own children. They are faced, as well, with finding ways to assimilate the children of either partner into their newly constructed households.[15]

How can men fulfill these expectations as fathers? How can we learn to grow as a result of our relationships with children? Part of the answer, I think, entails discarding some of our traditional attitudes of distance and autonomy. Parenting is not something that only a mother should do merely because she happens to bear a child. From the moment of a child's birth men can assume responsibility for nurturing sons or daughters and for sharing such nurturance with their wives. Some may argue that such commitment might put an unbearable strain on our work or upon our marriages. My response is that one must choose between constant striving at work and a more moderate path which would allow us to spend more time and energy with our children. Our employers might thus come to understand and accept refusals to make job transfers or to undertake schedules which create strain on family relationships. As recent research indicates, fathers can fruitfully expand their parenting skills and can learn to care for their children in ways which complement rather than merely reproduce the parenting of mothers.[16]

There are no easy answers to the issues raised by changed expectations of fatherhood, as there are none for other questions of changing masculinity. Many of us have experienced dramatic alterations in the ways we act as fathers, and increasing numbers of men will experience such changes in the future. We are faced with surrendering traditional models of masculinity, with giving up free time for the needs of others, with supporting our families in new and different ways, and with reevaluating our career directions. The rewards are great in terms of a closer connection with our children and the women in our lives. The price we pay, however, is a loss of the comforting conventional ideas we have about ourselves as men. Change disrupts our fixed universe and undermines a narrow and outmoded sense of masculinity. It stands to reason, however, that a real man is not one limited to being a financial provider and a source of strength in times of trouble. He is also a nurturer, a caretaker of his children, and a person sensitive to the needs of others.

POSTSCRIPT

While I was writing this book (in fact, while beginning this chapter) Sara and I learned that we would have a child. Conception required more time than we had planned, and as in my earlier experience with Rachel, I began to be assailed with doubts about my capability during the time of waiting and hoping. Despite what I had learned in my first experience with fatherhood, and despite my knowledge that conception often requires much time, I found myself beset by doubts akin to those of the past, as well as by the new fear that the passage of more than a decade had somehow decreased my abilities. Perhaps, in fact, I was condemned merely to repeat the dilemmas and anxieties which I once thought I had overcome.

During these anxious months I came to realize, however, that the quality of my response differed from that which preceded the conception and birth of my first child. My experience with Jake enabled me to thread my way through many of my fears and anxieties. Besides drawing upon past experience to help allay my worries, I was able to speak with Sara in ways which were impossible during my first marriage. She, too, had fears and she had feelings of guilt. At some moments, she concluded that perhaps she was not "entitled" to become a mother; occasionally, she worried that something had gone dreadfully wrong and that she was unable to conceive. Discussing our anxieties became an endeavor of listening closely and of finding ways to give and receive support. These moments were not easy, for they raised many anxieties about our future together. At times, we argued and almost against our will we traded mutual accusations. At other times, we were sad or we even joked (my aging sperm might need crutches to complete their journey; her eggs might all be cracked). In the end our sadness and laughter and our resolve to share our feelings were helpful, but it remained clear that being unable to conceive a child can put great stress upon a man and a woman and upon their relationship.

I was able, as well, to speak with other men about this situation. At first, I was reluctant to do so. Despite brave resolutions about being more "enlightened" and more "expressive" than men of an earlier time, I found it difficult to approach my male friends with my fears. When I was finally able to confess my anxieties, I found somewhat surprisingly that other men shared many of them. One man, soon to be a father himself, told me, "I had some real anxieties even before we attempted to conceive a child, and to deal with them I wanted to do fertility testing and get a sperm count right away. I wanted to see what the story was before we even started. It took us six months to get pregnant, and it was a time of tension. We finally decided to forget our previous timetable and to try not to worry so much, and that's when we conceived—we sort of snuck up on it." Another man noted that "I really didn't want to think about being unable to conceive a child. After we had started trying I wanted to block out my fears. But when we did conceive, I realized that I was very proud and that it meant a lot to me to be a man who was in good working order and who had a kind of magical power to bring about life. I felt good about myself, and I felt a real sense of relief, and I also felt scared that suddenly we were going to have a baby."

For me, these discussions with friends and with men interviewed for this book helped not only to lessen my fears, but to reconfirm my wavering belief in the power of sharing my feelings with others. Sara had found it easy to discuss her anxieties with her women friends, and again I marveled at the ability of women to rely upon each other for sustenance and support. I had difficulty doing this with other men who were close to me, but I eventually discovered (perhaps rediscovered is more apt) the value in seeing that others often feel as we do. Men have a common fund of experience and knowledge. Learning to draw upon that fund can be an important resource during difficult episodes in our lives.

Eventually, Sara and I went to see her gynecologist, a gentle and sensitive man, who advised us to be less concerned and to try less actively to conceive. We gave up counting fertile days on the calendar and charting Sara's variation in body temperature. Much as in the case of my friend quoted above, our more relaxed attitude soon had a positive outcome. Within a month we conceived a child, and we both breathed a sigh of relief. Besides feeling good about this new baby, I felt proud that I had learned from the past to cope with the present. I had repeated something of my experience of Jacob's conception, but I now had more ability to deal with fears of masculine failure. Such fears might still be present, but I could now confront them more directly and could see them as less than overwhelming.

Pregnancy is a time of joy, but of anxiety as well. Unlike the experience of having a first child, I can look forward to the birth of this infant with some understanding that a baby introduces changes into one's life. I can balance a sense of knowledge and some expertise against the desire for a novel and fresh experience in a new relationship. Above all, I feel less trepidation than I felt in first-time fatherhood. I know that given a modicum of good care, this new child will likely survive. The energy devoted to child care might seem sometimes to be wasted and the work might seem drudgery, but nurturing shared between men and women is ultimately of great importance to parents and children alike. The time spent in caring for a child has a shape and duration of its own, and, after all, children do not need their diapers changed forever. They soon grow from toddling to walking, from infancy to childhood, and then to adolescence and beyond. With succeeding children we can learn more about being fathers. We can share as men in parenthood.

Such feelings have received corroboration from another man who is presently looking forward to a second child. "I'm relaxed about being a father for the second time," he says. "As opposed to the ambivalence I felt with the first child, I find myself feeling excited and sort of mellow. I think about it during the course of the day, and sometimes I discover that I have a smile on my face."

"I know that I can now be my own person," he continues, "and as much as I am looking forward to a second child and to sharing the parenting with my wife, I realize that it is not necessary to allow a new baby to rule our life. We need our privacy and some distance from the children, and we each need to pursue our careers and to have time to ourselves. I used to feel guilty about such thoughts. Now I think that they're not so bad." I must say that it feels good to hear others express such sentiments, for these feelings are very similar to my own.

In thinking about having a new child, Sara and I also faced some questions which emerged from the particular nature of a second marriage. Sara is concerned that I might not love a child of our union as much as I love Jacob, and despite my assurances, I sometimes experience similar fears. I have fantasies, as well, that this marriage will somehow end as did my previous union, and that I will be left as a divorced father to two children by two different wives. Perhaps Sara's feelings arise from some anger that I have had a child in a previous marriage and perhaps they arise from her need to answer questions as a new parent that I have answered already: questions about whether she can care for our child as well as she has seen me care for Jacob. Some of my own fears stem from a lingering sense that shared parenthood will prove too great a drain on my time and energy and from anxiety that the resulting anger and frustration will lead us to serious conflict. Such issues remain to be confronted and, with luck, resolved. I cannot as yet report any definitive outcome nor would I want to do so. I can only say, "to be continued. . . ."

Notes

1. James A. Levine, *Psychology Today*, November, 1980, p. 112.
2. See *The New York Times*, Feb. 24, 1980, p. 20 E.
3. See Gregory Rochlin, *Masculine Dilemma* (Boston: Little, Brown and Co., 1980), pp. 20–21 about such fears and anxieties and about the potential for conflicted feelings introduced by fatherhood.
4. Sam Bittman and Sue Rosenberg Zalk, *The Expectant Father* (New York: Hawthorne Books, 1978); Alliance for Perinatal Research and Services, *The Father Book: Pregnancy and Beyond* (Washington, D.C.: Acropolis Books, 1981).
5. See, for example, Shelia Kitzinger, *The Complete Book of Pregnancy and Childbirth* (New York: Knopf, 1981), pp. 139ff.
6. Ross D. Parke, *Fathers* (Cambridge, Massachusetts: Harvard University Press, 1981), pp. 14–15; Alliance for Perinatal Research and Services, *The Father Book*, especially Chapter 6.
7. See Parke, *Fathers*, p. 24.
8. *Ibid*, p. 28.
9. See Rochlin, *Masculine Dilemma*, pp. 205–206ff.
10. See *Parke*, Fathers, p. 71.
11. *Ibid*, p. 44.
12. See *Ibid*, pp. 53–54; also see, David B. Lynn, *The Father: His Role in Child Development* (Monterey, California, Brooks-Cole, 1974), pp. 126–28, 14ff, 178–88, 268; Robert A. Fein, "Research on Fathering: Social Policy and an Emergent Perspective," in *The Journal of Social Issues*, Vol. 34, No. 1, 1978, pp. 122–35.
13. See Kristine M. Rosenthal and Harry F. Keshet, *Fathers Without Partners: A Study of Fathers and the Family After Marital Separation* (New York: Rowman and Littlefield, 1980).
14. See James A. Levine, *Who Will Raise the Children: New Options for Fathers (and Mothers)* (Philadelphia and New York: J.B. Lippincott, 1976), pp. 35ff.
15. See Rosenthal and Keshet, *Fathers Without Partners*. Andrew J. Cherlin, *Marriage, Divorce, Remarriage* (Cambridge, Massachusetts: Harvard University Press, 1981).
16. See Parke, *Fathers*, pp. 114–115.

CHAPTER 8

The Paradox of Masculinity

"Do I contradict myself?
Very well then . . . I contradict myself"
—WALT WHITMAN, *Song of Myself*

Men are undergoing major changes in their lives. In the past decade, the women's movement and some deep shifts in the social and economic environment have made us think differently about ourselves. Dual-career family patterns, the sharing of child care and house care, and a greater sensitivity to emotions and feelings have increasingly become part of male experience. Most men have been touched by these elemental changes, but none more than the middle-class men who have been the subject of this book. Some of these men—but not many, it appears—reject such changes outright. They do so at their own peril, for such a choice effectively isolates them from their contemporaries, both male and female. Other men—the great majority—respond in ways which can only be termed ambivalent. They support and sympathize with the women who may have pushed them to reconsider their beliefs and actions, but they also feel divided and uncertain, and at times they resist the changes occurring in their lives. They are caught, in other words, in the paradox of contemporary masculinity, suspended between the world in which they grew up and the one in which they must now live.

What might be the solution to this present-day male dilemma? There do not seem to be any easy answers to that question. We can, however, begin to chart the ways in which we might understand our divided feelings and thus attempt to deal with them. First, it is important to note that the ambivalence and insecurity about which we have spoken might now be considered a rather expected and almost normal aspect of contemporary experience. Instead of denying the existence of such emotions, it is important to be aware of them and of how they impinge upon our lives.

We might come to understand, as well, that it is perfectly all right to experience ambivalent emotions in regard to our sense of ourselves as men. Indeed, as psychologists from Freud to Erik Erikson have told us, ambivalent feelings often accompany the process of growth and can be taken as signs of health rather than decline. Such feelings, in fact, might now be seen as growing pains in the development of a new and more full masculinity, a masculinity which permits us at the same time to pursue our careers, to express our emotions, and to nurture our children. Our sense of insecurity and resentment does not necessarily render us sexist or anti-feminist. It might actually indicate the opposite—that we are individuals who are attempting to deal with change in our lives. Instead of opposing the gains that women have made, or blithely labelling ourselves as men who are somehow "liberated" (and thus without need to think further about such issues), many of us are attempting to understand the strains and difficulties which we now face.

It is important to realize, in addition, that the transition in our sense of ourselves as men might not soon be completed. It will require much time for men to adjust to new definitions of masculinity and to overcome their insecure and divided feelings. In the case of women the process of change has been an uneven one—from the initial success of demands for equality to the present blockage of the Equal Rights Amendment and the recent backlash against legal abortion and existing laws against sex discrimination. Men will most likely face an equally long and uneven road in the shift to a new sense of masculinity. Traditional definitions and behavioral requirements will not fade easily away, and our contradictory and ambivalent feelings will still be part of our lives, at times subsiding, and at other times becoming more pressing.

For most of us, the process of broadening our idea of what it means to be a man will most likely proceed in several phases. Indeed, as I consider the changes in my own sense of masculinity I am able to identify a number of distinct transitions. In childhood and adolescence I seized upon traditional images of masculinity, for these were safe (and they seemed the only models of manhood that existed). The image of the macho and powerful man who was in control of himself and his surroundings gave my contemporaries and me virtually all that we thought we needed to know about our emerging masculinity. In early adulthood I attempted to live out this version of malehood, but I was confronted at the same time by a variety of new ways to think about both men and women. While I still assumed that I could somehow aspire to be like John Wayne or Humphrey Bogart—someone dominant and sufficient unto himself—I learned the first lessons of the new women's movement. Suddenly, I was expected to share household chores and child care and to give up both my time and my own aspirations to help in the launching of my wife's career. Although I grudgingly honored most of these requests, I could not square past image with new reality. I harbored secret resentments which I brought to bear against Rachel, and my animosities about her changing expectations (and hers about my resistance) finally helped to doom our marriage.

Over the past few years I think that I have entered a phase which might be considered that of growing maturity. I have mostly come to surrender my earlier images of masculinity as unworkable and unrealistic. I attempt to share with Sara in all aspects of our life together. I now think that a man can be many things: a person who pursues work and career, who is a nurturer and a parent, and who is a friend to men and women alike. I have become ready to give up some of my aspirations to easy and safe dominance and to face the confusion that results from the demise of a comfortable and ready-made definition of proper male behavior. I am more able to voice my ambiguity and resentment and to tolerate uncertain and defensive feelings so to resolve differences which often emerge in daily life. I have been increasingly able to turn to other men for support, and I feel less threatened that in doing so I will be perceived by them as less than a man. While I do not claim to be any sort of model for other men (indeed, so many of us are engaged independently in similar struggles), I feel good that I have been able to make such changes in my life. I am hopeful, finally, that I will be able to transmit to my children the ability to explore some of these questions in less pressing and potentially less painful ways.

Today, masculinity is something other than it was only a short time ago. In earlier generations, both men and women were expected to accept virtually without question the existing images of what it meant to be an adult individual. The present no longer allows this luxury of a pre-ordained adulthood. We are now confronted by a series of contradictory models of what it is to be an adult and a person, a man or a woman. This state of affairs by its very nature produces deep anxieties. At the same time, it allows us to become what might be termed "self-created" individuals, people who are no longer defined merely by the images of the past, but who are increasingly able to develop our own beliefs and modes of action. Although we can at times revert to the stereotypes and attitudes of the past, we cannot rely on them as signposts to proper behavior. As men, we also lack a sense of an "enemy" which we must overcome in our efforts toward self-definition. At least women have been able to define themselves in distinction to men who supposedly oppressed them, and this has provided needed confidence in their struggle for change. Despite such difficulties, however, both men and women now have the opportunity to render themselves self-created adults, individuals who no longer need to depend so heavily upon inherited patterns and beliefs, but who can begin to strike out on their own.

This does not mean, however, that men and women will necessarily become alike and that eventually we might live in a world in which meaningful distinctions between the sexes no longer prevail. In an important recent book, Joseph Pleck, a well-known psychological researcher, has demonstrated the weakness of traditional and rigidly formulated models which define male and female behavior. He has indicated, in addition, that sex role stereotypes and norms are not psychologically innate, but that they are created by the expectations that society places on members of either gender.[1] Although sex roles are thus created by society, we should not expect that socially-sanctioned differences between men and women will quickly die out. I am convinced that for the foreseeable future we will not live in a world which is constructed along "unisex" lines—a world which does not seek to differentiate between men and women. Women will continue to bear children, they will perceive themselves as different from men, and they will continue to face problems rooted in past discrimination. Men, for their part, will contend with images of former dominance, and they will confront issues that centuries of power and privilege have left as a legacy.

What is important, however, is that men today broaden our repertoire of possible behaviors; that we begin to overcome our misgivings about our passage to a more self-originated masculinity; that we see this passage not as a loss but as a gain, and that we view it as a way to draw upon our untapped inner resources After all, if the range of approved personal behavior is ultimately defined by the society in which we live, then as members of that society we, ourselves, can help to broaden that range.

Several simple resolves might help ease our transition. It is important, first of all, to share our feelings and our difficulties with the women in our lives. Men have usually relied on women to massage our egos. We have often turned to them from a position of strength and this rather ironically has allowed us to feel dependent upon women for confirmation of our own self-image. Now, however, we might become able to share our feelings from a stance of great equality. This will allow us, in turn, neither to lord our masculine dominance over our female counterparts nor to rely on them to refurbish our waning self-confidence.

It is important, in addition, to make ourselves available for sharing household chores and personal tasks—everything from the daily dishes, to the childbirth experience, to the ongoing care of children. Many of us might reply that we already are responsible for such collective labor, and others might note that they do not care to contribute any more than their present quota of household work. Whatever our level of participation, I am convinced that the arena of daily life and of mundane chores provides the setting in which we will best be able to surrender our sense of male entitlement. It is also the location where we might deal most directly with the feelings of resistance and resentment which this entails. For most of us, the domestic scene is the place where we can come to experience ourselves immediately as new kinds of men—men who know both how to bring home the bacon and how to cook it once we get it there.

Attempting to be more expressive with other men is an additional step. Men traditionally have been reluctant to share feelings with other men for fear of losing prestige and a sense of masculine self-reliance. It still requires much effort to express our sentiments to our male contemporaries, and much of this depends on the setting in which we find ourselves. I think it difficult, for example, to talk about anything that pertains to emotions when I am at work, and other men have told me about an equal reluctance. We have jobs to complete, and we often cannot risk allowing our feelings to impinge upon work goals. I find it difficult, as well, to speak in any but the most conventional ways with men who are members of my softball team or with friends whom I might meet at the park for a run after work or for a pick-up game of ball. I am able, however, to speak openly with some of these same men if I talk with them personally on the telephone or if we go out for a beer together. Still, it almost always is more difficult to express my feelings to men than to women, and I often rely upon Sara to urge me to get into contact with my male friends. In this way (as in so many others) I feel myself a man in transition. I live between two worlds: one which seems at times unable really to fade away, the other not yet completely born.

What might the future hold in store? We must realize, I think, that the contemporary process of change is but the beginning of a long shift in the nature of our society. It is likely that the American economy will become increasingly reliant on advanced technologies such as microchip data processing, photo-voltaic cells for the production of energy, and the application of gene-splicing techniques in nutrition, medicine, and pharmacology. As this occurs, we will find that our definitions of work and leisure, of production and consumption, and even of life itself will continue to undergo alteration. The roles that men and women play and their ideas about these roles are bound to shift further in a world of rapid technological innovation—a world in which children might often be conceived outside the womb or in which men might be able to breathe a contraceptive spray from an aerosol inhaler. Despite the current efforts of traditionalists and conservatives to turn back the clock, we will most likely witness heightened change in the relationships between men and women and in the nature of the family over the next several decades.

In the foreseeable future, however, men and women will probably need to maintain dual-career households both for economic reasons and to attain a sense of mutual accomplishment. They will also need to depend on each other to share in the raising of children. Indeed, at the present we are witnessing what has been called a "mini-explosion" in birth rates as the offspring of the post-war baby boom begin finally to bear children of their own. In 1980, for example, there were almost two million more births than deaths reported in the United States, a higher rate of population increase than occurred for several preceding years. If such a trend continues we shall find that more çouples are faced with questions of how to juggle their jobs, the care of children, and the household chores.

It is probable that couples will seek to innovate in order to cope with this shifting environment. Such solutions as part-time work for both marriage partners, flex-time job schedules, and paid work leaves for fathers may become more common as families in greater number begin to seek such changes. It is likely, as well, that increasing numbers of men will be single parents or househusbands for some time in their lives. Investigation into the effects of flexible time schedules indicates that men and women on such schedules might not necessarily spend more time with their children and families. They seem, however, to experience less strain between the requirements of home and of work, and this raises the possibility that the quality of their contact with their mates and children might be bettered.[2]

At present, many of these innovations have been explored in several European (and especially Scandinavian) countries—societies which historically have had greater commitment to equality between men and women and to family-based social policy than our own.[3] It is not likely, however, that families, employers, and government in the United States will develop policies which might draw directly upon such European examples (since social innovations do not in the main seem directly transferable from one society to another). Instead, the process of redefining male and female roles and of reaching a *modus vivendi* between men and women who both work, who both nurture children, and who are both responsible for maintaining the home will no doubt evolve in a specifically American direction.[4] This will occur, I believe, because men and women who work and who raise families will require such changes from employers and from government. It will occur despite the current vissicitudes of a conservative political climate, a climate partially created as a desperate backlash against mounting demands for these very changes.

The final two decades of the twentieth century hold out the possibility not only of a more thoroughly technological society but also of a society which integrates some of the recent shifts in the perspective of men and women alike. This is a process that will not soon be completed. In the future, however, it will not seem very novel if a man works some of the time, takes care of children some of the time, shares his emotions and feelings with others, and if he feels substantially different about being a man than did his own father and grandfather. He will be on the way to resolving the paradox of masculinity and to achieving a "self-created" manhood—a manhood constructed more by choice than through the acceptance of the male symbols, rituals, and practices of a mainly outmoded past.

Notes

1. Joseph H. Pleck, *The Myth of Masculinity* (Cambridge, Massachusetts: MIT Press, 1981), especially Chapters 1, 9, and 10.

2. See Ross D. Parke, *Fathers* (Cambridge, Massachusetts: Harvard University Press, 1981), pp. 102–103; James A. Levine, *Who Will Raise the Children? New Options for Fathers (and Mothers)* (Philadelphia and New York: J.P. Lippincott, 1976), pp. 67ff, 87–91.
3. See Parke, *Fathers*, p. 103; Levine, *Who Will Raise the Children?*, pp. 91–93; Sheila B. Kamerman, *Parenting in an Unresponsive Society: Managing Work and Family* (New York: The Free Press, 1980), pp. 173ff.
4. See, for example, Levine, *Who Will Raise the Children?*, pp. 93ff; Kamerman, *Parenting in an Unresponsive Society*, pp. 121ff, 166–169.